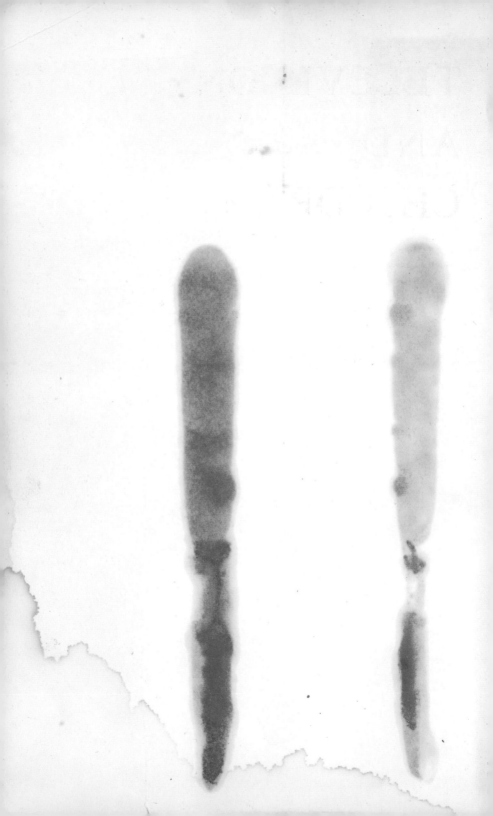

TELEVISION
AND
CHILDREN

TELEVISION AND CHILDREN

Michael J A Howe

Department of Psychology
University of Exeter

LINNET BOOKS · HAMDEN, CONNECTICUT

1977

First published 1977 as a New University Education Book,
an imprint of Clive Bingley, 16 Pembridge Road, London W11.
Simultaneously published in the United States of America as
a Linnet Book, an imprint of The Shoe String Press, Inc.

Library of Congress Cataloging in Publication Data

Howe, Michael J A
    Television and children.

        Bibliography: p.
        Includes index.
        1. Television and children. 2. Violence in television.
3. Television programs for children—Great Britain. I. Title.
HQ799.2.T4H68   1977   791.45'01'3   76-28991
ISBN 0-208-01537-X

Printed in Great Britain

CONTENTS

INTRODUCTION

As a psychologist I have learned to place little trust in my earliest memories, but I think that the year was 1946 and the programme 'Muffin the Mule'. I would have been six years old, and was staying with relations near Hastings. I clearly remember that around tea time our chairs were carefully arranged to face a large squarish box in one corner of the room, and after the blinds had been drawn the apparatus was switched on. We waited in silence for what seemed a very long time. Then we began to hear a buzzing noise, and, eventually, faint images started to appear on the glass screen of the instrument. The programme must have lasted for twenty minutes or so, after which transmission ceased, the set was switched off, curtains drawn back, chairs re-arranged and we returned to the activities of an ordinary afternoon.

That was my first experience of television. In fact, it was not then a particularly new innovation. It had been invented many years earlier, and from 1936 to 1939 the BBC had regularly transmitted programmes. Cup Finals had been televised, and so had Test Matches, the Derby, Chamberlain's return from Munich, a range of topics from gardening to comedy, and over three hundred plays. (1) The makeshift, almost amateurish nature of early television broadcasting—breakdowns were frequent, for example—together with the tiny screens, contributed to an absence of the striking qualitites of images encountered in film. Nothing I saw in the early days of television had the visual impact of 'The Wizard of Oz' or 'Bambi'. I don't remember anything I saw on television causing the nightmares experienced after seeing the horrifying film 'Pinocchio'.

I think it is still true that messages conveyed by television tend to be muted in force. Colour does add an extra dimension, but for most of us television retains a quality of domestic familiarity, perhaps even of cosiness. This familiarity provides the clue to the real cause of the long-term effects. Television's impact comes not from any particularly striking quality of the medium as such, but from the simple fact that it is present

7

all the time in the familiar environment of our homes, for much of the time switched on. The unique power of television as a medium through which we may be influenced in various ways lies mainly in the fact that we spend a great deal of time looking at it.

Nowadays, almost every evening when I get home from work I find that at least one of my children is watching television. Like most fathers I have from time to time wondered about the effects of long hours of television viewing on my children. On some occasions, the concern has briefly taken on a sharper edge. There was the time, for instance, while we were living in the USA, when during a holiday in rural Maine we pointed out an old graveyard to my three-year-old son. 'Who shot them?', he asked. Coming a few months after Bobby Kennedy's assassination, the remark, although shocking, was not altogether unexpected; but it did something to force me to recognise how the kind of world they live in can affect young children.

Television admits children to a world beyond their daily environment. It enables all of us—adults as well—to become aware of varieties of awareness and experience that were closed off to the parents of most of us. It has always seemed to me that television must be extremely influential, especially upon children, but as to the magnitude of its effects, and the precise form they take, I, like almost anyone, have remained blissfully vague.

In writing this book I set out to discover what hard facts are to be found concerning the effects of television upon children. Naturally, I looked for evidence about a number of different kinds of influence. The questions that have attracted most attention from both parents and researchers concern the possible effects of violent and aggressive acts portrayed via television upon children's behaviour, and upon their toleration of violence and their attitudes towards it. But of course there are other ways in which we might expect children to be affected by what is presented to them on the small screen that engages their attention for so many hours. What civilizing influences does television exert? What kinds of knowledge do children acquire from television, and how is their awareness of the world influenced? Do they learn new non-aggressive patterns of social behaviour, and to what extent do they acquire new interests and skills? Does television encourage a general trait of passivity? Furthermore, are children's attitudes to life in general, or to particular aspects of it, sport, religion, patriotism, politics or whatever, significantly influenced by television? Are sexual attitudes and behaviour affected? These broader questions, and the ones which
8

indicate possible positive effects of watching television, are of less obvious and immediate social concern than those which deal with violence and delinquency. Yet in the long run they are equally important.

Television on a large scale has now been with us in Britain for around twenty-five years, and in this time a great amount of research into its effects has been undertaken. From time to time most of us encounter newspaper reports or magazine articles describing the results of this or that research project, and occasionally the television channels themselves mention the findings of investigations. For most people, knowledge about the influence of television is based on such haphazard acquisition of piecemeal reports in the media. To seek for answers to the questions I have raised I have exposed myself to a fair amount of the research data that has been accumulating over the past twenty-odd years, and I have tried to take a hard, cool and systematic look at the findings, in order to discover what they add up to. What clear facts are available, and what statements can we make with reasonable certainty about the influence of television on children? For instance, is the link between televised violence and delinquency as clear as that between, say, smoking and lung cancer, or does considerable room for conjecture remain? I have also searched the evidence for answers to my questions about the positive influences. Are children better informed, more aware, more or less gregarious as a result of watching television? In short, what does television do to our children, the adults of tomorrow?

The outcome of my attempt to bring together the various kinds of evidence that research has made available concerning television's effects upon children comprises the major part of this book. As I expected, the distribution of research efforts directed to investigating the various kinds of anticipated influences turns out to be somewhat uneven. Thus, there is a vast amount of data about the effects of television violence, whereas knowledge about the positive outcomes of watching television is, to say the least, somewhat patchy. Some important questions remain unanswered because relevant research findings are too sketchy or non-existent. Some issues which have given rise to loud cries of alarm remain untarnished by evidence of a factual nature. For instance, whilst the more vociferous of those puritan individuals who claim to represent a silent majority would have us believe that televised references to sex do all kinds of harm to our young ones, I was hard put to it to find a single definite fact on the matter.

Having been engaged over the past ten years on research into human learning I came to this investigation with a number of presuppositions,

9

expectancies and prejudices. First, I have become strongly aware of the fact that children are different from adults in a number of non-obvious ways, which affect the outcome of exposure to any medium, including television. For example, their immature self-identification makes them less able than adults to distinguish between fantasy and reality, and therefore less well equipped to make a distinction between cartoon violence and violence in real life. At the same time children are likely to hero-worship and identify in one way or another with various screen characters. The sad fact that children have been killed by jumping off tall buildings, imagining themselves to be Batman, comes as no surprise.

My research into human learning has also heightened my awareness that no individual, even the youngest, is by any means a passive recipient of information. We attend mainly to what interests us the most and to what we can understand. These latter factors, themselves largely determined by our past experiences, make us selectively attend to some things, to ignore, forget or distort others which happen to clash with our preconceptions, and broadly speaking, to code and process the data that television makes available so as to make some kind of sense to each of us as an individual. It is commonly observed that any two people will give wildly differing accounts of events they have mutually experienced. This is often strikingly apparent when witnesses are asked to give descriptions of accidents or crimes that have occurred in their presence, and it is noteworthy that children are found to be notoriously unreliable as court witnesses.

The knowledge that each individual plays a highly active, integrative role in dealing with incoming information underlies one especially important consideration that must be taken into account in an analysis of the effects of television upon children. This is the simple fact that each child is unique. In practical terms, this means that we must be alert to various kinds of individual differences that may modulate the influence of any event. Thus we might expect to find that some children are more strongly affected than others by the portrayal on television of violent actions. If so, we would like to know what kinds of children are most vulnerable or 'at risk' in certain respects. We might expect to find, for instance, that a child who has little social interaction with other children and with adults, who does not read and who has few opportunities to participate in experiences of an educational or cultural nature would be more strongly influenced by what he sees on television than an individual who has a wide range of social activities and experiences, and whose parents sometimes discuss with him the programmes he watches. In
10

some of the research that has been undertaken into the influence of television, strong efforts have been made to take into account the differences between children. For instance, studies of the effects of television violence on delinquent and non-delinquent youths have carefully looked into individual differences. However, it is true in general that disappointingly few studies have systematically taken into account such differences between children.

Being a social scientist, I approached the available evidence with a wary eye for the possible activities of particular vested interest and pressure groups. That such an attitude of mind does not denote unreasonable suspiciousness on my part can quickly be confirmed by any reader who takes the trouble to look into the circumstances surrounding the publication in 1972 of the US Surgeon General's report on the impact of televised violence. Most of the scientists, who were commissioned to undertake the research summarised in the report, judged that sufficient evidence existed for it to be legitimate to make certain clear statements concerning a link between television violence and certain kinds of delinquent behaviour. However, in the summary report of the research that was widely publicised by large-scale publication and reported in the news media, the pressure on the Surgeon General's Scientific Advisory Committee by those members who were representatives of the television industry—the operations of which are largely determined by the profit motive—resulted in considerably 'toned down' conclusions, which appreciably qualified the views of the scientific contributors. Hence the statements about the research that were made widely available and were reported in the mass media were considered by the scientists to misrepresent their real findings.

These are some of my preconceptions, the considerations that were in my mind as I began to search for evidence. There is a further fact—a possible bias—which I ought to make clear at this stage. This is that on the whole I very much enjoy watching television. Perhaps childhood conditioning has made me a contented addict, for I can watch television programmes, including some of those which are undeniably trivial, without the feelings of guilt that friends and colleagues claim to encounter. The reasonably high esteem in which I hold British television has been influenced by my living two years in the USA, where I found television programming to be even poorer than I had been led to expect, and three years in Canada. If one wanted to say something nice about Canadian television standards one could always remark that they were higher than in the USA.

The following chapters deal with television's various influences on children. Chapter one starts by describing children's viewing habits—how

11

long they watch for and what they see. Of course, children do not watch only children's programmes and the chapter considers their preferences. Children's viewing habits differ not only in the amount of television watched, but also in content and in their reasons for watching television.

Television provides children with a 'window on the world', and chapter two discusses the kind of world that the viewer encounters. In some respects the world portrayed on television is true-to-life, and in others it is distorted. The chapter surveys investigations designed to discover whether children are seriously misled by the distortions, and considers ways in which a child's thought and reasoning processes influence his perception and understanding of messages conveyed via television. Television companies are aware of children's vulnerability, and some efforts are made to protect the young.

Chapter three describes what has been discovered about informal learnings that occur as a result of regularly watching television. What kinds of information do children retain, and in what respects are children who watch television better- or worse-informed than children who do not? Does television influence children's vocabularies? The chapter also describes research into the influence of television on a range of attitudes and interests. Experiments undertaken to compare what is remembered after watching colour and black and white television are described.

In chapter four we examine the available evidence about the ways in which television violence can affect children and adolescents. The alternative research methods include laboratory experiments, surveys and field studies, and each of these has certain characteristic advantages and limitations. The chapter also considers the different ways in which children can be influenced by violence. Increases in violent acts and delinquency are not the sole concern; tolerance of violence in others and attitudes to the use of violent means for achieving desired goals are also important. The evidence strongly points to certain conclusions about the effects of television violence, and their implications are discussed. The chapter concludes with an attempt to examine the effects on children of sexual content they encounter in watching television, the brevity of which reflects the lack of knowledge on this matter.

Television for children is discussed in chapter five. British television broadcasts a large number of high-quality children's programmes, but relatively little is known about the influence of these materials upon child viewers. An American field study investigating the effects of one programme designed for children is described in some detail.

12

Chapter six considers materials that have been produced for television with the deliberate intention to help children learn. In America the best-known instance is *Sesame Street*, which was conceived with flair and imagination, was carefully researched at all stages, and has had well-deserved success. The success of *Sesame Street* has encouraged and influenced the development of more recent American education ventures. Some interesting explorations have used 'dual-audio' television, whereby a second auditory channel gives young children information and explanatory materials designed to help them understand and gain more than might otherwise be possible from watching everyday television series such as cartoons and adventure programmes. In Britain, much, but certainly not all, of the efforts to help children learn from television have gone into schools broadcasting.

The final chapter includes some suggestions for dealing with problems that the survey of television's effects has brought to light.

On average, people in Britain, including children, spend something like two hours of every day watching television. This in itself constitutes a remarkable effect. Millions of people are spending so many hours of their lives in a manner which was inconceivable a generation ago, and during these hours they prevent themselves from following the various pursuits—sports, music, reading, writing, racing pigeons, work, sex, crime—that might otherwise have filled their time. As to the further influences of television, insofar as our children are affected, I have attempted to lay out the facts in the pages that follow.

A number of individuals have kindly aided me by helping to locate published materials. In this connection I would especially like to thank John Abel, Irene Shaw and the Inter-Library Loan staff at Exeter University Library. I also wish to thank Mrs Margaret Topham, who typed the manuscript with her customary skill.

REFERENCES
1 Black, P: *The biggest aspidistra in the world.* London: BBC Publications, 1972.

Chapter 1

CHILDREN AS VIEWERS

In a novel by the Polish-born writer Jerzy Kosinski (1), the young American central character has spent most of his life in isolation, and his knowledge of the world is based largely upon what he has seen on television. As he encounters people in a variety of circumstances his memories of television programmes provide the major guide to his actions and social behaviour. He refuses alcohol, because he knows that on television it can put people in a state they cannot control. He is confused when a woman flatteringly tells him that in some ways he is not really American, and more of a European man, since television has shown him the contrast between the polite, well-dressed and respectable people who refer to themselves as Americans and the hairy, dirty, noisy and disreputable individuals who admit to being un-American. He tries to work out the connection between a woman's private parts and the birth of children. Television series on hospitals and doctors and operations have shown him something of the mystery of childbirth, but they have given no indication why some women have children and others do not. When a girl makes sexual advances he is able to handle the situation up to a point, as he has learned from television that men and women seated together often approach very close to each other, sometimes partly undressed, and then embrace and kiss. However, he has no idea how to proceed from that stage, since on television what happens next is invariably obscured.

Some children's real circumstances are unhappily close to those of the hero of this fable, those who spend the largest amounts of time watching television tending to be the ones whose environments are the most impoverished, in the restricted range of experiences encountered and in their lack of social contact with other children and adults.

Time spent viewing

The vast majority of children devote fairly large amounts of time to watching television. Average figures should be treated with some caution.

14

since they tell us nothing about what any one individual sees, but they do provide a useful rough guide to viewing habits. As it happens, finding out how many hours the average child spends viewing is more difficult than one might expect. One way of acquiring information on this question is simply to ask viewers what they watched on particular days, or how long they spent viewing. This can be done by interviews or by asking respondents to keep a diary in which they report their viewing activities. Alternatively, it is possible to connect devices to the television sets of a selected sample of viewers. These provide an accurate and reliable record of the number of hours during which a set has been switched on, and, if necessary, the particular times at which it has been on. Such methods have shown that in Britain during 1971 every home containing a television set had it switched on for 5.2 hours, on average, each day. The corresponding figures for 1972 and 1973 were 4.8 hours and 5.6 hours respectively.

One might expect the alternative methods to yield closely agreeing measures of time spent watching television. In fact, this is not really so. Perhaps surprisingly, viewers' reports in diaries or at interviews often tend to exaggerate viewing times, overestimating the recording device's measures of the amount of time during which each set is switched on, and hence available for viewing. Figures showing the amount of time during which a television set was turned on may substantially overestimate the period of time during which it was actually watched. Experiments in which a camera was attached to television receivers in order to record when it was being watched have shown that American televisions, once turned on, may remain on over lengthy periods of time, like electric light bulbs, irrespective of whether any member of the family is actually viewing. In one American investigation the cameras attached to television sets recorded that only three hours of viewing occurred for every four hours that families reported in a television diary, and for every six hours they claimed to have been viewing when answering interview questions about what they had seen on the previous day. (2) While viewing television children were seen to engage in a range of activities including scratching, untying knots, throwing objects and nose-picking.

As people get more and more accustomed to having a television in the house, they become more likely to leave it on even when they are giving little attention to it. The term 'secondary viewing' is applied by one researcher to describe the circumstances in which television viewing forms an accompaniment to other activities, such as housework and reading. (3) About one quarter of the watching time of adult American viewers is spent in secondary viewing, the amount of such secondary viewing as a proportion of total viewing time being substantial only in countries with high television saturation levels. Almost three-quarters of the older children surveyed in one recent American study reported that they studied with the set turned on. (2)

Despite the various complications encountered in estimating how much time individuals spend watching television, the findings of a number of surveys and investigations are in reasonably close agreement, and indicate that, on average, the British child spends slightly above two hours per day watching television. The average number of hours per week watched by British adults and children over five years of age is around fifteen; seasonal and year-to-year variations being fairly slight. (4) According to the British Bureau of Television Advertisers, the average total weekly hours for viewing BBC1, BBC2 and ITV by adults and children over five were 15.7 in March 1972, 13.8 in August 1972, 14.8 in October 1972 and 17.1 in March 1973. Television is watched slightly less in the summer than in winter. The BBC reports that during the first three months of 1974 the average amount of viewing was 17 hours 51 minutes per week, and they state that this figure is below that recorded for the corresponding months of 1973. (5)

The amounts of time spent watching BBC and ITV programmes are broadly similar. It is difficult to compare figures issued by ITV and the BBC, because BBC statistics are based upon the responses to interviews in which individuals are asked to report what they have seen on television, whereas ITV figures refer to homes rather than individuals, and are based upon the amount of time during which a television set is switched on. The British Bureau of Television Advertisers' figures indicate that during 1972 and 1973 adults and children over five in Britain spent slightly more time watching BBC1 and BBC2 combined than ITV programmes. (4) However, ITV's figures indicate that during 1973–1974 fifty-six per cent of the total time for viewing television in homes was spent watching Independent Television. (6)

The figures for child viewers alone are roughly comparable with those for the total audiences. However, if we consider viewing by children during the weekday afternoon hours between 4.00 and 5.45pm, when there is usually emphasis on materials specially designed for child audiences, it emerges that young children are attracted to BBC programmes, and older children are more likely to watch ITV. (7) For the total age range five to fourteen years, my calculations from BBC figures for the first three months of 1973 indicate that twenty-seven per cent of the potential audience watched BBC, on average, compared with twenty-one per cent of the potential child audience viewing ITV at the same time.

16

Breaking these figures down according to age, it is found that among five- to seven-year-olds thirty-eight per cent watch BBC and eighteen per cent watch ITV. The comparable figures for eight- to eleven-year-olds are twenty-seven per cent (BBC) versus twenty-four per cent (ITV), and among children aged twelve to fourteen sixteen per cent were viewing BBC and twenty-two per cent were watching ITV programmes.

British children average about half-an-hour less viewing per day than the typical American child, and slightly more than the average times for most other European countries. On the whole, children spend more hours watching television at weekends than on weekdays, and there is some variation between children of different ages. Children tend to be slightly heavier consumers of television than adults, and the highest viewing figures are for the twelve to fourteen age range. It is likely that younger children would spend as much time viewing were it not for their earlier bedtimes. Boys and girls watch television for approximately the same amount of time in Western countries, but not in Japan, where girls view less, possibly because they are expected to devote a considerable amount of their time to household chores.

On weekdays, children's viewing takes place mostly in the afternoons, but a substantial number of young children watch television until the late evening hours. On an average evening, between 7:30 and 8pm forty-four per cent of Britain's five- to seven-year-olds are watching television, as are sixty-five per cent of eight- to eleven-year-olds and sixty-one per cent of children aged between twelve and fourteen. (7) Among the youngest group the percentage watching diminishes to thirty-five per cent for the succeeding half hour, then to twenty-two per cent, and by 9 to 9:30pm only seven per cent of this age group are still viewing. However, quite a large proportion of these children remain viewing until 10.30–11pm, by which time the number watching, although only two per cent of the age group, remains large in absolute terms. Naturally, a larger proportion of older children stay up late, and among the eight- to eleven-year-olds, for instance, fifty-three per cent are watching between 8.30 and 9pm. In the next half hour the figure drops sharply to twenty-seven per cent, but thirteen per cent are still viewing after 10pm. The viewing figures for the children aged between twelve and fourteen do not begin to drop substantially until 9pm, and then decline relatively slowly. Thirty-three per cent are still watching between 10 and 10:30pm and eighteen per cent watch during the following half hour.

Children's enjoyment of watching television is strongly influenced by time and occasion. In a British study undertaken for the Independent Broadcasting Authority (8) children were asked 'What do you most enjoy

17

doing?' at three separate times. These were 'after you come back from school', 'on Saturdays and Sundays' and 'on holidays when you don't go to school'. Their responses showed some striking differences between these occasions. Preferences for most of the chosen activities, such as playing with friends, playing football and reading, did not vary much between the three alternatives. However the choice of 'watching television' was strongly influenced by context and time. About thirty-one per cent of the children chose watching television as their most enjoyed activity for the part of the day immediately after school, while only eleven per cent chose it for weekends, and a mere five per cent chose television as the most enjoyed activity for holidays. Doubtless a number of separate factors contribute to these differences, but the pattern of findings does strongly suggest that children like television most when they are relatively tired and feel a need for relaxation.

Other members of the family are often present while children are watching television, especially at weekends, and this may influence the content of children's viewing. As one might expect, the amount a child views is strongly related to the length of time his parent spends watching television. A British investigation undertaken in 1958 showed that only one per cent of the heaviest viewing of three groups of children had parents who viewed little, whereas sixty-three per cent of these children had parents who were themselves heavy viewers. There is no reason to suppose that this state of affairs has changed substantially in recent years.

Individual differences in viewing habits

Viewing figures are related to social class, and children whose parents are relatively wealthy and well-educated view, on average, half-an-hour less per day than children from families in the lowest socio-economic classes. (9) Recent survey findings (2) indicate that class-related differences are now less pronounced than they were in the late 1950s, but one recent survey shows that American university graduates spend only about half to two-thirds as much time viewing as less well-educated people. (3) In Japan the negative relationship between television viewing and ability, measured by intelligence tests, holds for fifteen-year-olds but not for younger children. Changes in an individual's place of residence or life-style can very strongly influence viewing habits. In a recent American study comparing viewing by university students and high school students from broadly comparable home backgrounds it was found that the high school students spent four times as much time watching television. (10)

18

The association that is found in Britain, America, and Japan, between high amounts of viewing and low educational levels seems to reflect an emphasis on popular entertainment in programme content. In eastern Europe, where there is much more stress on serious and educational programmes, better-educated people watch more television than those who have less education. (3) This does not appear to be due solely to differences in wealth, which might influence ownership. In both Britain and America highly educated people have tended to lag behind others in the purchase of television sets.

What kinds of children watch television the most? A number of investigations have looked for evidence of personality differences between heavy and light viewers, and some reliable findings emerge. One problem which arises when it is demonstrated that viewing habits are associated with personality differences is that of deciding whether there are any causal links involved. That is to say, do the personality factors influence the amount of time spent watching television, or vice versa, do both influence each other? It is quite possible that any such relationship is due solely to additional factors, in which case neither personality attributes nor viewing habits directly influence the other. Questions of this kind become especially important when we have to consider the survey evidence to be encountered later in the book concerning the effects of viewing upon children. At this stage we simply need to make the point that correlations or relationships which are found to exist between personality variables, on the one hand, and viewing habits, on the other, do not necessarily constitute evidence that television influences personality. There is often a greater likelihood that viewing habits are influenced by viewers' personalities, which in many respects are relatively stable and enduring, than that personality is fundamentally influenced by viewing.

Among children, heavy viewers tend to differ from light viewers in a number of ways besides those directly related to social class, intelligence and school achievement. On the whole, British and American studies agree in finding that children who for one reason or another are socially insecure, or who do not have satisfactory relationships with their families, or with other children of similar age, are likely to be heavy users of television. (11) For them it appears to serve as a kind of retreat, a haven from some of the frustration of real life. High viewing levels in children are associated with conflicts and maladjustment between children and parents, and in particular the kinds of conflict, perhaps more common in the United States than in Britain, caused by the parents setting higher levels of aspiration for their children than the children themselves accept.

19

This kind of conflict may result in the children seeking mass media outlets having a strong fantasy component, for instance, in comics and 'confession' pulp magazines as well as television. In general, young people who during adolescence are relatively light viewers of television and read more than the average tend to put greater emphasis on the use of television as a means of acquiring information than other young viewers. Those who continue during adolescence to spend a great deal of time watching television are found to use it largely for entertainment. The latter group can be characterised as 'seekers of fantasy', whereas the adolescents who spend less time viewing tend to choose activities more closely attuned to reality. (11)

One interesting study has shown that there is an association between heavy viewing and strong conventionality in American adolescents. (10) The authors rated the extent to which high school students were 'psychologically involved' with television, using an index based upon scores for exposure to television, the perceived importance of television to them and the perceived influence of television. Those individuals in whom psychological involvement with television was rated as being high were found to have patterns of thought and action that were conventional in that they closely conformed to the established norms, traditional majority values and expectations of adult society. Compared with lighter viewers they tended to place more value on academic success. They were also less tolerant of abnormality and deviance, and less critical of the current state of the world. Their political opinions were less liberal, and their attitudes towards the use of drugs more negative, but they were more religious. However, the actual behaviour of the adolescents who were highly involved with television was not totally in accord with their expressed attitudes. Their use of marijuana was less than that by the light viewers, as one might expect, but their scores for other forms of generally deviant behaviour, based on measures for lying, stealing, and fighting, were no lower. Thus it appears that involvement with television tends to be associated with somewhat rigid, authoritarian attitudes, but not with noticeably virtuous patterns of behaviour.

The tendency for children who have difficulty in forming social relationships to be heavy viewers of television is present from early years of childhood. It is found, for example, that six-year-old boys who watch much television are more likely to engage in solitary play than light viewers, and although physically more active they are passive in interpersonal situations, less responsive and less attentive. (2)

20

The amount of time a child spends with television is not determined solely by the child himself, and in most cases it is affected to some extent by parental controls. A minority of parents, around one third, impose definite rules that restrict the hours when their children can watch. More often, parents invoke sporadic controls, directing which programmes their children may watch or forbidding viewing at a particular time. Of course, parents' preferences influence choice of channel, and thus provide one source of control over what children actually see. (12) In a British investigation undertaken on behalf of the Independent Broadcasting Authority (8) it was found that almost a third of all parents denied that they ever tried to stop their children watching any television programme. Among those parents who did claim that they sometimes prevented their children from viewing, by far the most commonly chosen reason was that it was too late for viewing, but twenty-seven per cent of the reasons these parents gave were related to the amount of sex in programmes, and twenty per cent of their reasons concerned violence on television. On the whole, parents in lower social classes were found to be more permissive than wealthy parents, but working class parents who did limit viewing were more likely than the others to claim that the reason for their preventing children watching some programmes was because they contained too much sex.

Solitary viewing by children is the exception rather than the rule, a fact which tends to go against the frequently made suggestion that television functions to a considerable extent as an 'electric babysitter'. In a British survey whose findings were published in 1974 children were asked to recall what they had seen on the previous day, and then questioned about the first programme they recalled. Only fourteen per cent of the programmes they mentioned were reported as being viewed alone. (8) Furthermore, it was the older children, in the twelve- to fifteen-year-old range, who were most likely to watch television on their own, and solitary viewing was most common among children from higher social class backgrounds. Neither of these findings gives any support for the claim that 'babysitting' is a major role of television. In fact, among the youngest children in the sample, aged five to seven years, on only nine per cent of occasions was the first-recalled programme watched alone. The data suggest, although not conclusively, that this figure would be even lower among children from lower social classes, for whom the babysitting function of television might most often be expected to operate. Doubtless many mothers look gratefully on television as a way of entertaining and occupying the minds of their offspring, but the research findings make it appear

KILLING TIME

very unlikely that the presence of a television set in the home actually diminishes the amount of contact between parent and child. This research also serves to demonstrate the difficulty of trying to investigate children's television viewing as a phenomenon on its own, since it actually takes place as part of the variety of activities that jointly contribute to family life. A report issued by Granada Television (9) shows that time and content of viewing by mothers and their children are very closely related, and the authors stress the fact that television viewing is one among many strands of family life, and is itself affected by many other things that make up the experience of day-to-day living as a family.

The published figures which show the average amount of time that children devote to watching television give us some indication of the extent to which they are open to its possible influence. American social scientists have quoted estimates of the total number of childhood hours that the child spends in front of the tube, the average figure being in the region of 15,000 hours. (3) This is more than the total amount of time each child spends at school or in all other leisure-time activities combined. Such statistics are indeed disturbing, both as an indication of the manner in which children cut themselves off from alternative activities (a matter to which we shall return) and as a measure of the extent to which they may be affected by whatever they are shown. However, the amount of time we devote to a particular activity does not necessarily provide a perfect measure of its influence. Most adults can think of work or leisure activities which have involved huge amounts of time without influencing them profoundly. For instance, at school I spent many hundreds of hours learning to translate prose from Latin into English and back again, but almost all I learned has been forgotten. It may be unfair to compare the effects of a distateful activity such as learning Latin with television viewing, which children enjoy and choose to do. But even pleasurable events are not necessarily influential. To choose another personal example, I can remember as a child of around ten spending many summer hours watching cricket, with enormous interest and enthusiasm. Today, however, my knowledge of the game and interest in it have both departed, and I would find it difficult to supply the names of a couple of players in the current England team.

Viewing preferences

This brief survey of children's viewing habits has shown that television engages a large proportion of most children's leisure time. How important an influence the medium is depends also upon what they see on television and how they react to it. We can discover something about the kind of information that television presents to children by finding out what children watch, and the nature of their preferences. The particular items that children view vary from one year to the next, but yearly variations in the kinds of programmes transmitted are small, and the preferences of children at a given age are relatively stable over the years. What a child actually sees on television is dictated partly by the programming policies of the television companies or networks, and partly by the individual child's likes and dislikes. Since television authorities all try to cater to children's interests, it comes as no surprise that the contents of children's viewing closely match their stated preferences.

Viewing preferences are affected by a number of separate factors, not the least important being age. A study undertaken by the BBC Audience Research Department (7) shows that some programmes are popular with British children of all ages. Examples are *Dr Who, The World of Disney, Blue Peter, Jackanory* and *Star Trek.* Some children's series are widely popular with children of all ages, such as ITV's *Black Beauty,* and the same is true of some serials, an instance being the BBC's *David Copperfield.* Even the youngest children enjoy some programmes made for adults or 'family' audiences. For instance, in the spring of 1973 Cilla Black's programme *Cilla* was watched by twenty-nine per cent of children aged five to seven years and thirty-eight per cent of all older children. Over the same weeks *This is Your Life* was also seen extensively by children of all ages, and this is also the case for *Top of the Pops.*

Amongst the youngest viewers, aged two years to four years, items specially designed for the young attract very large audiences. On an average day viewing figures for programmes such as *Watch with Mother, Play School, Crystal Tipps, Magic Roundabout, The Wombles, Rainbow, Hickory House* and *Mr Trimble* hover around fifty per cent of all children in the age range. Except for *Watch with Mother,* which is shown during school hours, programmes of this kind are also popular with the five- to seven-year-olds, and amongst these children during 1973 programmes such as *Crackerjack, Deputy Dawg, The World of Disney, Right Charlie, Blue Peter, Basil Brush, The Brady Kids* and *Scooby Doo* were all likely to attract audiences of around half the population. A large number of these children also watched evening transmissions aimed at older viewers. For instance, thirty-six per cent watched the *British Film Comedies* series and a similar number saw *Top of the Pops,* both being shown at around 7pm.

23

The BBC figures for the spring of 1973 show that among eight- to eleven-year-old children *The World of Disney* attracted about sixty per cent of the viewing population. The children's programmes watched by the younger viewers were also popular with this group, and between a half and two-thirds of them watched additional children's items such as *Lollipop Cover, Mr Mole,* the children's news transmission *Newsround,* and *Val Meets the VIPs.* They also viewed in large numbers some programmes occurring later in the evening, including *Morecambe and Wise, The Fenn Street Gang, Cilla, Alias Smith and Jones, Whatever Happened to the Likely Lads, Now Look Here* and *Some Mothers Do 'Ave 'Em.* Some materials were watched distinctly more often by children in this age group than by either older or younger children. Examples are *The Virginian, Morecambe and Wise,* the BBC film series *High Adventure, Star Trek* and the *British Film Comedy series.*

For children between twelve and fourteen *Top of the Pops* was the most popular television show in 1973, and it was watched by two-thirds of the young people in this age group. Otherwise the trend is naturally towards watching more of the programmes seen by adults, although some children's programmes such as *Blue Peter* and the series *Black Beauty* were watched by around a third of these children. In this age group items such as *Opportunity Knocks* and *The Fenn Street Gang* were also successful in gaining viewing figures of above forty per cent.

Amounts of television violence
Stating the names of television programmes young viewers watch helps indicate some of the content to which children are most frequently exposed. The question concerning programme content which is most often asked by parents and others concerned about the kinds of events portrayed on television, is, how much violence do young children see? This has been asked repeatedly over the years, and at least since the early fifties the short answer has been, quite a lot. On the whole, the amount of violence on British television has been somewhat less than in the USA, but more than in some other countries, such as Israel, where the average number of violent episodes per programme is about a sixth of the number shown in the United States, and Sweden, where there is very little television violence at all. (13)

One report of British television transmissions, covering programmes broadcast in the later afternooons and evenings of spring 1971 (2) showed that there was an average of four violent incidents per hour during the period 4pm—11pm. This compares with a figure of seven violent incidents

24

per hour on American televison over a similar period. Cartoons were by far the most violent programmes, having as many as thirty-four violent incidents per hour. Interestingly, five of the six cartoons seen on British television in this study were American-made. It was also found that many other programmes containing high levels of violence shown on British television were of American origin. Almost forty per cent of programmes imported from America were based on crime, action and adventure, but only half this percentage of programmes made in Britain were of this kind.

Another report of programme contents, published by the British Broadcasing Corporation (14), gives somewhat lower figures for the average number of violent incidents per hour. The difference is probably due to variations in the criteria adopted for scoring events as being violent. The BBC figures refer to broadcasts by all three British channels between 4.40pm and the end of transmissions during the period November 1970– May 1971, except for a three-week gap at Christmas. This study assessed the number of 'major incidents' of violence, as assessed by five trained monitors who watched each programme. On average, 2.2 major incidents of violence were observed per hour, that is 1.3 per programme. There was more violence on weekends than weekdays, and on the former a third of all programmes contained three or more violent incidents. Perhaps surprisingly, the amount of violence on the three alternative television channels was very similar, as was the proportion of incidents resulting in fatalities and the number including intended physical violence. On all three channels about fifty per cent of programmes contained no violence at all. Many of the violent events occurred in dramatic fiction programmes, a category which includes Westerns, police and detective features, spy thrillers and other 'adventure' series. However, many of the violent events, 'not far short of half the total number' according to the BBC report, occurred in news or current affairs programmes. The results of this study confirm the observation by other investigators that, on average, US programmes shown on British television contained twice as much violence as home produced features. Thus, a third of all US programmes contained four or more violent incidents, but this is true of less than one in ten British programmes. Among the most violent features shown during the period covered by the report were *Mannix, The Untouchables, The Virginian, Star Trek, The Baron, I Spy, Hawaii Five-O, The Avengers, Dr Who* and *Callan*. All but the last three of these are American. Among these noticeably violent programmes, we have already noted that *Dr Who, The Virginian* and *Star Trek* figure prominently in the lists of items watched by large numbers of child viewers.

Attitudes to television violence

It would be quite wrong to assume that the substantial amounts of violence shown on British and American television are forced upon unwilling viewers who would really prefer to see less violent features and series. Programmes that contain highly violent episodes are often very popular among both adult and child audiences. The popularity of material of this kind is indicated equally by viewing figures and by the findings of surveys of viewers' attitudes to alternative kinds of television content.

Many British families, perhaps most, do not regard television violence as an issue of any importance at all. In a BBC investigation (14) fifty families, each consisting of mother, father and up to three children were invited to have dinner at Broadcasting House and to take part in a relaxed discussion about television. The intention was to use this informal situation as a means of finding out about the impact of television violence in the everyday lives of typical viewers. The researchers were rather surprised to discover that very few of the viewers spontaneously mentioned violence at all during the discussion, unless the BBC researchers brought up the subject themselves, and they concluded that for most viewers violence on the television is simply not a salient issue. Following the discussion over dinner the participating families were shown a film from a crime series names *Vendetta,* and this contained a large number of violent incidents. However, even after seeing it, the families rarely introduced its violent aspects into the discussion, without appropriate probing.

Survey results provide additional evidence that most viewers in Britain are not overly concerned about violence in particular programmes. A substantial proportion of adults do agree with the general proposition that 'there is too much violence on television nowadays'. Forty-one per cent of viewers aged under thirty and sixty-three per cent of viewers over thirty agreed with this statement. However, when asked to view a sample of seventeen programmes, mostly containing some violence, with around three violent incidents each (ie about twice as much violence as the 'average') only twenty-five per cent of those respondents who were aged under thirty and sixteen per cent of those aged over thirty classified the actual programmes they saw as being 'very' or 'quite' violent. Furthermore the apparent indication of concern about violence was by no means reflected in the attitudes of viewers towards particular features. In fact there was not even any close relationship between the number of violent incidents in a show and the number of participants who judged it to be violent. For instance, fifty-one per cent of the viewers who saw a programme called *Sovereign's Company,* containing a grand total of two

26

violent incidents rated it as being 'very' or 'quite' violent, yet only seventeen per cent gave equivalent ratings to *The Sinking of the Bismark,* which contained as many as seven violent incidents. No association existed in the adult respondents' responses between the amount of violence individual programmes contained and the adults' assessments of their suitability for children. For instance, the episode of *Star Trek* which participants watched contained considerable violent action inflicted by fists, guns and solid objects. A female crew member was struck in the face, and apparently suffered considerable pain, yet this episode was ranked as being suitable for family viewing by the overwhelming majority of viewers participating in the study.

The behaviour and attitudes of children themselves similarly indicates considerable liking for some of the programmes which contain high levels of violence. Not only do children choose to watch in large numbers those programmes most highly saturated in violence, such as *The Virginian, Star Trek, Mannix, The Baron* and *I Spy,* but they also list the quality of being exciting as a chief reason for liking their favourite programmes. Among older boys, excitement is the most favoured quality, whereas girls most often choose the attribute of being funny as their chief reason for liking programmes. (8) The highly violent American cartoons shown on British television are popular among children of all ages.

Some American investigators have reported associations between social class membership and preference of violent or adventurous programmes. Younger and less able children tend to show a greater preference for programmes based on fantasy rather than reality. (15) However, the most recent research findings appear to indicate that among British youngsters social class differences in preferences are small. (8) Age differences are more striking, young children aged between five and seven years, especially girls, often choosing the funniness of programmes as the chief reason for liking them whereas, as we have noted above, older boys of all social classes find excitement the major attraction. It apparently takes some years to acquire a taste for violence.

Among British boys and girls there is an association between viewing preferences and delinquency. (16) Juvenile delinquents on probation have a greater liking for aggressive and violent television programmes and less preference for educational and informational materials than nondelinquent individuals of comparable age and intelligence. Furthermore, the delinquents more often state a liking for or indicate interest in the 'heroes', suggesting a greater tendency to identify with the characters in violent programmes.

27

Some reasons for watching television

Why do children choose to watch television? When asked, they gave a variety of reasons for viewing. In an investigation undertaken in 1972 (17) boys and girls wrote an essay about 'Why I like to watch television'. Children of all ages quite often listed simple relief from boredom as one reason for viewing. As one child put it, 'Sometimes I get bored with everything so I turn on the TV'. Some children mentioned using television as a means of refuge, for instance 'For keeping out of trouble', or 'Getting away from the rest of my family'. Others listed television viewing as a means of forgetting school, home work and other problems. The fact that television can help us learn about things was mentioned by a number of children, and some of them said they valued television as a way of finding out what is going on in the world, or learning things that are not taught in school. Some children looked on the medium as a means of learning about themselves and discovering how to act in various situations. Others expressed reasons for liking television that were related to its arousing functions, and children often mentioned the thrilling and humorous aspects we have already discussed. The function of helping with relaxation was mentioned by a number of older children, but younger ones rarely remarked on this. Some children valued the medium for companionship, one sad individual stating 'It helps me forget I'm alone'. Equally pathetic were the responses of a few children who showed abnormally intense positive responses towards the television. One child said 'If I had to give up the television, I don't know what I'd do', and for another 'Life without TV would not be worth it'. Such remarks have a sharp edge that is obscured by the more restrained tones of the research reports which comment that excessive involvement with the medium is an indicator of poor adjustment. (15)

Among older children in Britain it is, perhaps surprisingly, the more intelligent who most often report using television as a means of avoiding problems. (18) Intelligent fourteen-year-olds also use television extensively as a 'coin of exchange' in conversation. There are a number of differences in the use made by the mass media in general by different categories of children. At the age of fourteen, for instance, less intelligent children are more likely to read comics than their brighter peers.

Children in Britain exhibit a high degree of consistency in their viewing preferences. A sample of ten-year-olds were shown a list of sixty programmes and asked to indicate whether they had seen each one and to rate it on a five-point scale from 'It is one of my favourites' to 'I don't care for it'. (15) After their preferences had been assessed in

28

this manner, the scores for those thirty-four out of the original programmes which had been seen by at least eighty per cent of the children were submitted to a procedure known as 'factor analysis'. This provides a way of classifying and analysing data, to yield 'factors' or 'dimensions' which indicate the attributes that tend to go together. In this instance the different programmes 'loaded' to varying extents on the factors which emerge from the analysis. The results of the factor analysis indicated that children who showed a strong liking for say, *Gunsmoke*, very often also liked other Westerns, such as *Laramie* and *Bonanza*. Similarly, children who stated a liking for *Juke Box Jury* also liked *Top of the Pops, Ready Steady Go, Thank Your Lucky Stars* and *Sunday Night at the Palladium*. Other kinds of programmes, such as quiz programmes, sport, science fiction and 'human interest' serials (eg, *Compact* and *Emergency Ward Ten*) clustered together in a similar manner. These findings make it clear that most children do have quite definite individual preferences for programmes of particular kinds. The items they report liking best by no means form a random or indiscriminate selection from the total sample they were asked to assess.

As one might expect, these consistent preference patterns were not unrelated to children's social and psychological characteristics. For example, it was found that the pop music programmes, which were liked both by boys and by girls, were especially popular with working-class children who rated low in academic achievement and who were more oriented towards teenage culture than to the values of the educational establishment. Among the ten-year-old respondents preferences for some programmes produced specifically for children (eg, *Five o'clock Club, National Velvet*) and for Westerns were associated with low ability, low need to achieve, and high fearfulness and anxiety, a combination of personality attributes which indicates intellectual and emotional immaturity.

This brief survey of viewing patterns and preferences has shown that there is a fair amount of violence on British television, and that although many adults agree with the broad statement that there is too much violence they do not appear to be very concerned about violence in the particular programmes which children view in large numbers. Young viewers have varied likes and dislikes. Younger children are enthusiastic about programmes that are funny, and older children especially like adventure series, which are often highly charged with violent action. Children watch television for many reasons, including boredom, loneliness, and the need to escape from problems. Their consistent preferences for particular kinds of items are related to a number of social and psychological factors.

Children's likes and preferences partly determine what each individual watches. In the following chapter we shall give closer attention to this aspect of television, that is, the actual content of viewing. Television introduces the child to a world outside his direct everyday experience. What kind of a world is it that television portrays? How authentic is it as a representation of reality and in what respects does it provide a reliable guide to real life? In what ways does it falsify life and provide a distorted picture of the world which might mislead the immature viewer as to the ways and means, the morals, conventions and rules of human existence, and is the child seriously misled when television does give a distorted image of the world?

REFERENCES

1 Kosinski, J: *Being there.* New York: Harcourt Brace Jovanovich, 1971.

2 Atkin, C K, Murray, J P, and Nayman, O B: The Surgeon General's Research program on television and social behavior: a review of empirical findings. *Journal of boradcasting,* 16, Winter 1971–72, pp 21–35.

3 Robinson, J P: Television and leisure time, yesterday, today and (maybe) tomorrow. *Public opinion quarterly,* 32, 1969, pp 21)–222.

4 Bradshaw, S: Daytime television. *New society,* 24, 1973, pp 429–430.

5 *BBC handbook 1975.* London, BBC, 1974.

6 *ITV guide to Independent Television.* London: Independent Broadcasting Authority, 1975.

7 *Children as viewers and listeners.* London: BBC, 1974.

8 Wober, M: Children and television. *Independent broadcasting,* 2, November 1974, pp 4–7.

9 Aitchison, D R: *What children watch: a report on a Granada survey of children's television viewing.* London: Granada TV Network, 1966.

10 Weigel, R H, and Jessor, R: Television and adolescent conventionality: an exploratory study. *Public opinion quarterly,* 37, 1973, pp 76–90.

11 Schramm, W, Lyle, J, and Parker, E: *Television in the lives of our children.* Stanford, California: Stanford University Press, 1961.

12 Leifer, A D, Gordon, N J, and Graves, S B: Children's television: more than entertainment. *Harvard educational review,* 44, 1974, pp 213–245.

13 Liebert, R M, Neale, J M, and Davidson, E S: *The early window: effects of television on children and youth.* New York: Pergamon Press, 1973.

30

14 Shaw, I S, and Newell, D S: *Violence on television: programme content and viewer perception.* London: BBC, 1972.

15 Harper, D, Munro, J, and Himmelweit, H T: Social and personality factors associated with children's tastes in television viewing. Appendix B of *Television Research Committee second progress report and recommendations.* Leicester University Press, 1969, pp 55—63.

16 Halloran, J D, Brown, R L, and Chaney, D: A summary of an exploratory study of the television viewing habits of adolescents placed on probation by the Courts. Appendix A of *Television Research Committee second progress report and recommendations.* Leicester University Press, 1969, pp 50—53.

17 Greenberg, B S: *Children's reasons for watching television.* BBC Audience Research Report. London: BBC, 1972.

18 Smith, D M: Some uses of the mass media by 14 year olds. *Journal of broadcasting,* 16, Winter 1971—72, pp 37—50.

31

Chapter 2

THE CHILD AND THE WORLD OF TELEVISION

If television enlarges a child's world it is likely to be a major influence in his life. A major concern is that children may believe what they see on television to be an accurate guide to reality when it is not. I would not for one minute suggest that all television *ought* to be realistic or true-to-life. Indeed, many of the adventures and romances that bring the greatest delight take place in what is very much a world of their own. The Western, for example, evokes a way of life that is highly structured in many respects, governed by a number of strict rules and conventions, in which cowboys are brave, shopkeepers are timid and good people are good. Characters' lives are strongly constrained by their roles. Only in a Western could the following dialogue take place. It is from *My Darling Clementine,* and goes something like this.

Man entering saloon, to barman: 'Hey feller, you ever been in love?'
Barman: 'No mister, I bin a bartender all my life.'

If television were simply to mirror the realities of life, a stated concern about the medium's influence would simply amount to an expression of concern about the quality of life in general. However, if it falsifies reality and shows children a distorted view of the world the influence of television may be more pernicious. In particular, the combination of an untrue picture of reality on the medium and a child's belief that what he sees there is true-to-life might lead the young child seriously astray. Yet however numerous the hours that a child spends watching television, his own actions and attitudes are unlikely to be strongly affected unless he thinks that television does portray life as it really is.

Television and real life

In this chapter we shall first examine some of the contents of television programmes, to determine whether major distortions and falsifications do occur, and later consider evidence of children's beliefs and opinions about the truth and reality of what they see. After surveying the world

32

of television we shall turn to the child's world, and observe how each child's interpretations of what he sees on television are determined by immature thought processes. Finally, we shall have some words to say about television companies' attempts to protect children from the possibly harmful influence of materials to which their inexperience makes them vulnerable.

Television violence needs to be examined in this light. Since it is conceivable that the violence seen on television has an influence upon child viewers, we ought to be concerned about the contexts in which it occurs, and about the forms which violence takes. For instance, assuming that children identify with screen heroes, it would be useful to know whether 'good guys' are likely to resort to violent means of achieving their ends, or whether violent acts are committed mainly by villains. Do the good guys only resort to violence as a means of preventing disastrous alternatives, or do they regularly use violent acts in order to achieve a variety of desired goals? Also, is the probability of acts of violence being successful higher when the motives for violence are reasonable and legitimate than when screen characters' aims are unreasonable, immoral or illegal? It is important to be able to answer questions such as these and to know how violent action and its uses are regularly portrayed in the world of television. Television not only has the important function of bringing the child to ranges of events and experiences that lie outside the environment with which he is in direct contact, but it exerts its influence at a time of life when the child's knowledge of the rules and conventions that govern social actions and moral behaviour is incomplete and immature. We would therefore expect that what television programmes portray to the child— especially, but not only, to the youngest viewers and those who view most heavily—about the kinds of acts that are acceptable and likely to bring prestige or material rewards in contexts outside the familiar environment of school and family, might be very influential.

The nature of violence on television
The recent BBC report on violence in television shows that almost half of all the major characters in dramatic fiction programmes shown on British television during the survey period were involved in some form of violence, either as victims or aggressors or both. (1) Ten per cent killed other characters, and an equal proportion died violent deaths. Forty per cent were victims of violence and one third themselves acted aggressively. Figures for BBC and ITV transmissions are broadly similar, but ITV characters had a somewhat greater likelihood of being violently assaulted,

33

fatally or otherwise. Although violence is much more prominent on American than British programmes, deaths are fewer in the USA, reflecting the policy of American television networks by which 'killings', but not non-fatal violent incidents, are severely restricted.

Most instigators of violence on television are young males. They are likely to be on the wrong side of the law in some respect, although only about thirty per cent are clearly classifiable as criminals and outlaws. Characters who did not act aggressively were usually rated in the report as 'good', 'honest' and 'kind' rather than 'cruel', but over half of the aggressors were also rated by viewers as being 'good', fifty-five per cent as 'brave', and seventy-one per cent were considered to be 'strong'. On the whole, heroes behaved less aggressively than villains, three-quarters of all bad or villainous characters being violent. This was three times greater than the proportion of heroes who were violent. On television, 'good' characters are very much less likely to be killed than villains, by a factor of almost ten to one. Good and bad characters also differed in their reasons for committing violent acts. In the case of the villains, fifty-two per cent acted aggressively for no just reasons, and another thirty-five per cent were acting under orders. The proportion of good characters who committed violent acts for no just reason was lower, seventeen per cent, but clearly this is by no means a negligible figure. Aggressive and non-aggressive characters differed in their goals and aims. For instance, killers appeared to be intent on self-preservation (fifty-four per cent) and acquiring money and goods (thirty-two per cent). Unaggressive characters tended to have goals with a strong social element, the well-being of home, family and society, and respect of the law often being considered important.

The outcome of being aggressive on television differs between the short and the long time-scale. On the whole, individuals who started acts of violence were more likely than non-aggressors to be successful in the incident during which the violence occurred, 'good' aggressors being much more likely to achieve their aims in the short term than 'bad' violent characters. However, in the long run those who acted violently were no more likely than other people to be successful, as seen by the final outcome of the programme.

The distinction between good and bad characters in dramatic fiction series made for children was more black and white than in the adult programmes, the villains being more villanous and the heroes braver and more altruistic. As the author of the BBC report points out, the distinction between good and bad characters on television becomes less clear as the evening wears on.

The British research on television violence is supplemented by the findings of an American study in which the investigators set out to show whether approved methods of achieving aims were more likely to be successful in television programmes than 'disapproved' methods, often involving the use of violence. (2) It was found that approved methods were in fact no more successful than methods such as illegal activities, violence and escape. In other words, in the world portrayed on American television ways and means that are not acceptable in the real world are seen as having as good a chance of bringing about the characters' goals and intentions as methods which are socially approved. This conclusion was found to hold for a variety of children's and adults' programmes, and the authors of the study emphasize the possibility that, as a result, children who watch considerable amounts of television may come to believe more and more in the necessity for using illegal and violent methods in order to succeed.

The findings of both these studies of television violence make it clear that the characters who are portrayed as heroes in programmes watched by children resort to violence quite often and achieve various kinds of success as a result of it. We have also noted, earlier, that children see a large number of violent actions on television. Taken together, these findings show that television gives a disturbing portrayal of life, but one which might be justified if it can be said to reflect the realities of human existence. To what extent is the violence portrayed on television realistic in its quantity, form, and in its depiction of the kinds of individuals by whom violence is committed?

We do not expect the world of television to provide a mirror image of everyday existence. Children and adults expect television to show them something different, something new. The choice is not simply between fantasy and escape, on the one hand, and on the other a slavish reflection of the viewer's own life. Nor should we wish to exclude all forms of fantasy and distortion that are violent, grotesque, horrifying or even obscene. Those who defend television against the criticism that there is too much violence frequently refer to such blood-soaked morsels as Macbeth, Titus Andronicus or Grimms' Fairy Tales, correctly reminding us that the classical repertoire of mythology, legend, folk-tale and drama is replete with every conceivable kind of horror, lewdness and bestiality. If Greek heroes can fuck their mothers and eat their children, so the argument goes, what's wrong with a little old-fashioned sadism in tonight's Western? It is a fair question, but in answer it should be made clear that a distinction can be made between the effects on children of events which are occasional and the effects of those which take place regularly and frequently.

Research into child development has shown that the major determinants of socialization are not, in general, sudden happenings, however dramatic or bizarre, but the kinds of habitual events that form familiar and constant aspects of the child's environment over a lengthy period. The possible danger of heavy exposure to violence on television does not lie in any particular event or scene that is portrayed, but in the child's lengthy and frequent exposure to the medium. The outcome of a child spending a good deal of his leisure-time watching programmes that incorporate a false or distorted view of the world, and using what is portrayed in them as a basis for knowledge and a model for his own behaviour could be destructive and dehumanizing. If children are not sufficiently well-informed to be aware of the manner and extent of television's distortions, we ought to be highly concerned about programme contents, Titus Andronicus notwithstanding.

Whenever there are systematic distortions in the way in which television introduces areas of life which are relatively important and for which the medium provides a child's sole or major source of information, we have to consider its possible ill-influences upon inexperienced young minds. We clearly need to know just how dependable is the picture of the world that television provides? Now that we have considered the context of television violence it is possible to assess the accuracy of its presentation of violent action and aggression. After assessing the extent and nature of television distortions, in its portrayal of those aspects of life and death in which fighting and shooting are encountered, we shall move on to examine the representation on television of a broader range of non-violent human activities. We can find out whether marked discrepancies exist between the ways in which various human roles and activities are depicted on television and their form in real life. Such discrepancies could mislead children in harmful ways. When we have established what possibly harmful distortions are present in the content of children's viewing we shall next ask whether they are *aware* of such distortions, and consider how children actually interpret the messages that television conveys to them.

There are some striking differences between television series and real life in the kinds of crime that are committed. For instance, American television crime is usually unsuccessful, ninety per cent of crimes being solved, whereas the comparable figure in real life is about twenty per cent. (3) (This is one of the very few television falsifications which might conceivably be justified on social grounds.) The discrepancy between crime in real life and in television drama can be illustrated by ranking the
36

various major categories of crime according to their order of occurrence. In the United States burglary is the most common crime, followed by larceny, car theft, robbery, assault, rape and murder, in that order. Murder on television, far from being last on the list, is first, assault is the second most frequent television crime (but fifth in real life) and it is followed by robbery, car theft, burglary (the most frequent crime in reality), larceny and, finally, rape. Only the latter, which occurs sixth in actual life and seventh on television, occupies similar positions in the two rankings, between which there is a negative correlation.

On an average day the British or American child who watches television for around three hours is likely to see twenty-odd violent incidents. This alone amounts to a huge distortion of real life. Doubtless modern living is becoming increasingly violent, but even in the United States the chances of an individual being a victim of real violence were estimated in 1967 to be only one in four hundred per year. (4) On television, unlike life, almost all criminals are involved in violence. (5) In the real world the majority of crimes involve money and property; very often the criminal and the individual whose belongings are stolen never see each other at all. Again, real police officers comparatively rarely fire their guns or inflict physical damage on criminals. But on television, over the years 1967–1969 US law officials acted violently on around seventy per cent of their television appearances. (5)

There are a number of additional ways in which the image that television gives of the role and scope of violent and criminal activities in society is highly misleading. For instance, in life, murders amount to a tiny proportion of the crimes reported to the police. The vast majority of homicides are committed by individuals who do not have a criminal record and quite often involve the murderer's spouse, lover, family, or people he has known for some time. On television, as a recent American report has shown, murder and mayhem are most likely to occur between strangers or near strangers. (6) In an average week of US television series only seven per cent of crime victims were hurt by members of their family, whereas in life almost a third of all violent crimes occur in a family context. (3)

Distortions in the portrayal of life
Distortions multiply as one passes from crime and violence to televised versions of a broader range of human situations. One American commentator has claimed that television teaches us that consumption, preferably conspicuous, provides the great measure of happiness and personal satisfaction, that success is signified by the purchase of products, and that

leaders and heroes come from among the physically attractive, the glib, the wealthy, and almost no-one else. (7)

Women get a very poor deal from television. Although women comprise around half of the population, only about twenty per cent of television characters are women on programmes shown in America (6) and about thirty per cent in dramatic fiction programmes shown on British television. (1) Women in drama series are more likely to be objects of victimization than are men, emphasizing their subordinate role in society, and they are less likely than men to inflict violence. (8)

The depiction of women on commercials is especially offensive. Germaine Greer has drawn attention to the large number of advertisements in the mass media for 'things to squirt on women to stop them from being so offensive'. (8) Television advertisements, especially in America, depict women as homebound housewives who very rarely have jobs. If a woman does have an occupation it is almost always of a subservient nature, and female lawyers, doctors, business executives and scientists are conspicuously absent from commercials. The woman's most frequent role is that of a decoration and sex object, and she almost never demonstrates the slightest hint of intelligence, independence or initiative. Happily, there is often a competent male around to tell the hopeless woman how to shine her floors or make her linens whiter than those of the almost identical housewife next door. Little girls who watch television commercials get a somewhat discouraging view of the range of roles and opportunities that will be open to them in adult life.

An American study has provided a systematic examination of the manner in which television content distorts reality in one important aspect of modern living, that relating to jobs and occupations. (9) Previous research had shown that seventeen per cent of the jobs depicted on television were connected with television work, and a similar proportion of the characters are criminals. (3) The authors point out that systematic and objective information about people's occupational status and roles is noticeably lacking from formal school education, and television therefore becomes a potentially-inportant source of the knowledge the children require in order to acquire the knowledge required for making realistic choices concerning their own occupations in adulthood. At present, for many children television may well provide the richest source of information about roles and occupations in the years preceding their joining the labour market.

The study investigated young children's knowledge of three distinct categories of occupation. The first of these, 'personal contact'

38

occupations, included jobs with which the ordinary American child comes into contact during his normal everyday life, such as teacher, owner of a small grocery shop, postman and school caretaker. The second category of occupational roles consisted of those which children were likely to see portrayed on television. These included judge, lawyer, reporter, head-waiter and butler. The third group of roles were called 'general culture-occupations', which the investigators considered to be widely understood by adults but rarely seen by children, either face-to-face or on television. Examples of these were shipping-clerk, hospital orderly, skilled printer, accountant and electrical engineer.

The authors discovered, as they had anticipated, that personal contact occupations were best understood by children, television contact roles coming next, and the 'general culture' occupational roles were least well understood. Television has a definite role in transmitting occupational knowledge. Thus the television contact occupations were better understood than the general culture roles, although they were no more visible to children in real life. Also, children who watched television most frequently gained higher scores than children who watched infrequently, in the test of knowledge about television contact roles. This was the case for the other job categories. In other words, knowledge of job occupations portrayed on television was enhanced by heavy viewing, whereas knowledge of the other job categories was unaffected. Another finding was that children of seven years and over, when asked to order the various jobs in terms of status and prestige, ranked television contact occupations both more consistently, as measured by degree of agreement, and more similarly to adults, than the other kinds of occupations.

The findings of this study show that television provides a more powerful source of knowledge about occupational status than either personal contact or the general culture of the child's neighbourhood. However, child audiences received stereotyped and highly uniform television portrayals of occupations. Lawyers were shown as being very clever, artists were temperamental and eccentric, policemen were hardened and often brutal, private detectives were resourceful and clever, nurses were cold and impersonal, and journalists were callous. The stereotyped nature of television portrayals was considered to have a homogenizing effect, tending to reduce individuality among television audiences. The investigators who undertook this study came to the conclusion that television provides children with superficial and misleading information about the labour force of their society, from which they acquire stereotyped beliefs about the world of work. Since occupational roles are important both for the individual and for the form that society is to take, a source of knowledge which distorts reality concerning this aspect of the social structure may contribute to personal and social problems. Findings such as the present ones also remind us that we need to be concerned about the possible contribution of television to a 'mass culture' which may eventually 'erode our moral convictions, reduce us to bland uniformity or brutalize our aesthetic sensiblities'. (9) The present results support those obtained from studies which directly investigate the effects of television upon children in indicating that television does provide an important agency of socialization for children.

The matter of occupational roles portrayed in dramatic fiction seen by children on television does not appear to receive much attention from broadcasters. However, in its *Annual report* for 1973–74 (10) the BBC claims that it has long wanted to develop 'more series and serials that break away from the routine theses of doctors and police'. Yet none of the three cited instances of such developments, *Warship, The Onedin Line* and *Colditz,* appears to do much towards providing undistorted insights into the nature of modern life.

Are children aware of distortions?

The evidence indicates that television projects to children a highly distorted view of the world, and does nothing to allay the suspicion that some children may be misled about important aspects of life in the twentieth century. The next question is, are they actually misled? To what extent are children aware of differences that exist between reality and what they watch on television? And, what kinds of children are likely to be led astray?

In some respects many young children exhibit a degree of scepticism and apparent sophistication in their assessments of the validity of television materials. By the age of twelve years, for example, only twelve per cent of American children agree that commercials tell the truth 'always' or 'most of the time', whereas two-thirds of them believed that television news is truthful most of the time. (11) Younger children are more likely than older viewers to judge television contents as accurately representing reality. Thus thirty-seven per cent of twelve-year-olds compared with only a quarter of sixteen-year-olds believe that characters portrayed on television are always or nearly always like people they meet, and nearly half the six-year-olds agreed that television characters are 'just like' or 'pretty much like' people the children personally know. Black American children and those from other minority groups are more likely to perceive televison programmes as being true-to-life. Social class factors are also involved. One American report concluded that forty per

40

cent of poor black children and thirty per cent of poor white children
were ardent believers in the realistic nature of television contents, compared with only fifteen per cent of children from white middle-class
families. Adolescents and children did not perceive violent programmes
as being any less real than non-violent ones (5) and forty-six per cent of
American adolescents agreed with the statement that crime programmes
tell about life the way it really is. Delinquent boys and those who were
rated as being aggressive were more likely than others to perceive the
violence in drama series shown on television as being realistic.

The situation undoubtedly warrants concern. Television does distort
reality, and many children do perceive what they see on television as being
closer to real life than it really is. Therefore, we can definitely expect
that some children, in particular those for whom heavy exposure to television is combined with an absence of alternative forms of experience and
social interaction, will acquire a distorted understanding of the way things
really are.

How children understand the world

What more can we say about how children perceive the messages on the
television screen? Up to this point we have had little to say concerning
children themselves except as viewers and users of television. A broader
consideration of some aspects of childhood can provide some additional
insights into their perceptions of what they watch.

One easily apparent way in which children differ from adults lies in the
restricted body of experiences they have available to form a base or yard-
stick by which to relate, judge and integrate newly arriving information.
I remember, at the age of five, being about to set out on a long car journey,
and hearing the word 'roundabout' inserted several times into the conversation. To me this word referred only to things encountered in fairgrounds,
and I became increasingly disappointed as the journey drew to its end with
never a fair in sight. Many adults can recall similar childhood events in
which lack of existing knowledge led to misunderstandings of information
newly seen or heard, and the autobiographies of individuals with sharp
childhood memories can often provide us with insights into childhood
awareness that are in some respects as illuminating and as relevant to our
task of trying to understand how young children perceive what they see
on television as are any of the findings of experts in the psychology of
child development.

Among psychologists, Jean Piaget is the scholar who has made the most
valuable contributions to our understanding of the child's world. Some
of his writings are highly theoretical, and concerned with hypothesized

41

structures and operations involved in epistemological competence, that is to say, the acquisition and possession of knowledge. However, Piaget has also managed to obtain a large body of down-to-earth observations of young children, and through talking to them and watching them perform at ingeniously-designed tasks he has gathered a great deal of knowledge about the young child's developing view of himself and the world around him.

Piaget has found that the world as experienced by the young child is highly concrete and closely bound to the surface appearance of things. The child's thinking is tied to perception, and some of the interpreting and abstracting operations that adults automatically and quite unconsciously carry out as they experience events are noticeably absent. Thus, asked to decide which of two objects is larger or smaller, the child makes a judgement that appears to be based on a comparison involving only one of the perceptual dimensions shared by the two objects. The child does not seem to be aware that the task requires him not only to take into account more than one dimension at a time, but also to perform a further mental operation, or 'reasoning' upon them. Thus the child of, say, four or five years of age, is frequently unsuccessful when asked to say which of two differently shaped jars contain the greatest amount of liquid. His mental processing is not so much wrong, in the sense of his making an error, but simply insufficient. His conception of the task as one involving only a simple perceptual comparison results in the choice of a method of solution which comprises making one simple measurement of length or breadth. Because the chosen method of solving the problem is inadequate, the answer is very likely to be incorrect.

On other occasions children's concentration upon the surface appearance of things may result in the retention of items that are rapidly forgotten by adults. One psychologist (12) describes a family outing by car to buy some rose bushes at a nursery garden situated in an unfamiliar countryside location. A year after their first visit, the family decided to return to the nurseries to buy some more roses. The father could remember the approximate distance and general direction, but he could not recall any specific landmarks, and was about to give up the search when his six-year-old son saw the correct turning, which he recognized immediately, with no shadow of a doubt. The child had retained a highly specific, concrete, perceptual detail, which contrasted with the more generalized and abstract scheme of things that the father remembered.

Designers of television programmes for young children do often take into account the concrete quality of children's thought processes, and

42

the visual nature of television contributes to its effectiveness in communicating to the young. One aspect of children's thinking that is not always easily apparent is its highly egocentric nature. Immature thought is closely centred around the child himself, and objects and people can only be conceived insofar that they related rather directly to the child's own experience. There is no conscious awareness of being 'selfish' in the adult sense. The most extreme forms of egocentrism are seen in young babies. In one of Piaget's experiments he observed that immediately a ball with which an infant was playing disappeared from sight the infant appeared to forget it completely, becoming completely unaware of its existence. Quite literally, out of sight was out of mind. The young infant is only aware of things outside him when he is in direct perceptual contact with them, and he simply has no comprehension of a world that exists apart from and independent of himself and his activities.

As children get older their egocentrism diminishes, but understanding of objects and people not directly in contact with oneself remains highly restricted. The child finds it very difficult to imagine how things appear from a perspective other than his own. For instance, shown a model of a mountain and asked to show how it would appear from a position other than that in which he is standing, the child of around six years performs less well than most adults expect him to, and the young person of this age is not fully aware of the fact that other people, and indeed other things, do not share all his experiences. Thus the child's thinking is 'animistic', inanimate objects being regarded as imbued with human feelings and motivations. The Sun, like the child, gets up in the morning, and shines when he is happy. Jack Frost and the North Wind and the Man in the Moon are all partly human in the young child's conception of things.

An outcome of the child's egocentric, animistic thinking is that he is very poor at distinguishing fact from fantasy in what he sees on television. This contributes to children's low level of awareness about television's distortions. We have previously referred to the fact that children have come to grief imitating the more dangerous activities of characters such as Batman. One six-year-old American boy is reported to have asked his father for real bullets, because his little sister 'doesn't die for real when I shoot her like they do when Hopalong Cassidy kills 'em'. (13) Some young children even appear unable to recognize the difference between cartoon characters and humans. One child seriously asked an adult who would win if Superman and Mickey Mouse had a fight.

Children's egocentrism also serves to provide a limitation on moral development. Young children first learn that particular behaviours are

43

prohibited, and gradually acquire a body of generalized and abstract standards in the form of rules which determine what the individual should or should not do. A striking difference between children and adults lies in the extent to which judgements of the rightness or the wrongness of a deed are based upon the consequences of the action, rather than the intention behind it. Thus an error by which a child's ball comes to break a greenhouse pane may be seen as far more blameworthy than an unsuccessful attempt to kill one's younger sister. Normally, most children advance from the stage in which consequences are seen as being all-important in determining the morality of acts, and by the age of about twelve years the child becomes able to make moral judgements which do take into account the specific situation in which a rule has been transgressed, and the reasons underlying a 'wrong' action.

A disturbing aspect of some television programmes is their presentation of situations in which the depicted relationships between intentions underlying acts of violence and the outcome of these acts would appear to work against rather than for children's moral development. For instance, as we have previously mentioned, research has shown (2) that in situations involving television characters who act violently, their behaviour is as likely to be successful in achieving its intended immediate outcome when the intention is antisocial as when the intention is good and morally justifiable. If children do perceive actions on television drama as providing an adequate guide to what is appropriate and justifiable behaviour in real life—and we have already seen that many of them do, in large measure—and if the television contents are used to provide models to be imitated, consciously or not, in their own behaviour, and examples which come to influence their own attitudes and view of life, there is little doubt that some of the programmes shown on television will have a negative influence upon moral development.

Underlying the specific differences between children and adults to which we have drawn attention, child thought is broadly distinctive in its relatively uncomplicated and incompletely differentiated nature compared with adult reasoning. This simplicity of thought processes certainly contributes to vulnerability. Children tend to think in terms of binary distinctions, things being good or bad, black or white, all or none. In one study an adult talked to four-year-old children about their conceptions of life as they saw it on television. (14) The children's responses included statements that the people on television are either all good or all bad, that all the cowboys are good people and all the Indians are bad, and that bad people bleed, but not good people. Furthermore bad men never do

44

anything that is good, and it is the job of cowboys to kill bad people and Indians.

The four-year-olds in this study did not have to search for reasons for killing. They said that all the good people have to kill the bad people. All the heroes kill only the bad guys, and you can't really talk to a bad guy— you must shoot him. Views about fighting were equally uncomplicated— the bad guys always started the fight, a gun means you are strong, and only the good guys should have a gun. As far as the children's own lives were concerned, the lessons taught on television were clear and simple. Every good person loves little children. To protect children, he must kill the bad people. If bad people try to hurt you, call your mother and she will get a gun and kill them.

These are the assembled statements of a number of four-year-olds, not the view of a single child, and some children at this age may be beginning to understand that differences exist between the conventions of televised Westerns, which they report so accurately here, and real life. Nevertheless, and granted that the four-year-old mind is one in which moral absolutes are dominant, it is hard to disagree with one expert (14) who considers this particular television-induced division of life into good guys and bad guys to be both sinister and dangerous.

At this point we can take a step back from the fairly massive array of evidence considered in this chapter, and give some brief answers to the questions that were raised. Yes, television does provide a world view that is highly distorted. Yes, some of the falsifications and distortions are indeed ones whose acceptance by children as being accurate representations or reality might seriously affect the growing child's view of the world. Yes, children do believe that what they see on television is a more accurate copy of reality than it really is. Research into child development has shown that there are a number of less than obvious differences between child and adult reasoning, and they contribute to the child's greater vulnerability to misleading television contents. Some children are more seriously misled than others, but the majority of children accept some glaring distortions as real. If we accept the notion that the view of the world which a child acquires constitutes an important component of socialization processes—a basis for attitudes and a guide to actions—we cannot escape the conclusion that children are influenced, sometimes harmfully, by the content of their television viewing.

Further evidence of the influence of television will be introduced in the next chapter. We shall then examine the findings of investigations which have taken a more direct approach to the problems, measuring the specific

45

outcomes of watching television. This will make it possible to develop the reasoning underlying our present conclusions and to add greater precision to our knowledge of television's influence.

Providing for vulnerability

Before closing the present chapter it is necessary to say something about the attempts made by television broadcasting companies to take into account the vulnerability of child viewers. To what extent do broadcasters and networks accept a responsibility to children? In all countries awareness exists that children need some form of protection, but there are large differences in the extent and manner by which this concern is reflected in the implementation of controls over programme contents. In the United States over many years little more than lip service has been paid by the television networks to the expressed need to protect children from injurious influences. Over the past two decades there have been numerous expressions of concern, reports have been commissioned and presidents have announced expensive commissions. However, with some notable exceptions the quality of US children's programming has remained low, and characterised by large amounts of violence.

Most other countries, including all of Europe, have done somewhat better. In Britain, both the BBC and the independent television companies belonging to the Independent Broadcasting Authority impose controls which make some explicit provision for the vulnerability of children. Over the years the BBC, for example, has taken its responsibility to protect children from harmful influences very seriously. It appreciates that in the absence of unacceptable censorship only limited protection is possible, and that part of the responsibility for ensuring that children are not exposed to possibly harmful programmes must be shared by parents. A 'watershed' policy is followed, by which most programmes deemed unsuitable for children are transmitted after 9pm, although the BBC does recognize that some children will be viewing after that time. (15) The ITV companies have a similar policy. They too realise that substantial numbers of children remain in the audience after this time, but consider that after 9pm parents should assume the responsibility for what their children see.

So far as violence is concerned, the BBC and ITV each operate a 'Code on violence'. The BBC code was most recently revised in 1972 (1), and the one used by ITV companies was prepared by a committee set up in 1970. (15) The BBC warns its television producers against setting undesirable examples which can easily be copied, such as using bottles in

46

fights or locking up 'prisoners' in cellars and empty rooms. There should be no dwelling upon the details of fights, and violence should be avoided in contexts which relate to child viewers' own lives, and invoked only rarely as a solution to a fictional situation. The ITV code points out that insecurity is less tolerable for a child than for a mature adult, and can easily be caused by scenes of domestic friction. It states that while violence shown as happening long ago or far away may seem to have less impact on the viewer, it remains violence, that horror in costume remains horror and that no evidence exists for 'sanitized' or 'conventional' violence being innocuous, even if the consequences are concealed or presented in a ritualistic manner. Furthermore, it warns, violence is not inevitably physical, and verbal acts can also convey violence.

How consistently the television companies follow their own rules and advice about the use of violence is a matter of opinion. A glance at actual programme contents suggests there may be greater laxity in allowing violent content than in allowing children to witness alternative kinds of materials which are considered harmful. For instance, BBC radio producers are expected to guard against disc jockeys playing pop records which contain 'references to drugs or drug-taking, obscenities or explicit references to sex' (15) when a substantial number of children are known to be in the audience. This taboo is imposed despite a lack of any real evidence that mentioning such things is harmful to children. On the other hand, where violence is concerned, the BBC considers that excluding all scenes of violence from television would falsify the picture of life presented to the audience and would also involve suppression and censorship. The truth of the matter, as we have shown, is that the picture of life presented in programmes the BBC regularly transmits is indeed exceedingly falsified, not by an absence of violence, but by a surfeit of it. Were the BBC actually to exclude almost all scenes of violence—as is undertaken by Swedish television— the view of life presented would in fact be far more accurate, and less distorted or falsified that it is at present. Furthermore, the avowed concern not to falsify the picture of life presented to the viewers is contradicted by the restrictions the BBC places on such themes as family insecurity and infidelity. To the numerous children who now inhabit one-parent homes, and who are affected by problems of marital discord, separation and divorce, the absence of marital difficulties in television programmes can hardly be reassuring. When one sees some of the disgustingly violent cartoons that are apparently considered suitable for viewing by the youngest children, one begins to wonder whether the order of priorities is somewhat askew, in the implementation of controls to protect children from harm.

47

To criticize the BBC too strongly is to attack a responsible organization for contradictions which are to some extent unavoidable when one tries to put into practice a programming policy that attempts both to provide some protection for children and also to be as open and varied as possible. Quite rightly in my opinion, the BBC bases programming decisions to a large extent upon what licence-paying viewers want to see, rather than exclusively upon what is considered good for them by the broadcasting authorities and producers. We have to remember that children and adults do enjoy and do choose to watch those programmes that contain violence. In a society which values freedom of choice and which for better or worse chooses to allow the media to cater to mass interest and tastes, any television company which aims only to educate and elevate its viewers, and not to entertain them as well, will end up by simply alienating them, thus losing its audience and discarding its potential to do good. Nevertheless, while the awkward fact remains that potentially harmful materials continue to be transmitted, parents cannot happily accept the existing state of affairs.

REFERENCES

1 Shaw, I S, and Newell, D S: *Violence on television: programme content and viewer perception.* London: BBC, 1972.

2 Larsen, O N, Gray, L N, and Fortis, G: Achieving goals through violence on television. In Larsen, O N (ed) *Violence and the mass media.* New York: Harper and Row, 1968, pp 97–111.

3 Dominick, J R: Crime and law enforcement on prime-time television. *Public opinion quarterly,* 37, 1973, pp 241–250.

4 Shulman, M: *The least worst television in the world.* London: Barrie and Jenkins, 1973.

5 Liebert, R M, Neale, J M, and Davidson, E S: *The early window effects of television on children and youth.* New York: Pergamon, 1973.

6 Leifer, A D, Gordon, N J, and Grave, S B: Children's television: more than entertainment. *Harvard Educational review,* 44, 1974, pp 213–245.

7 Johnson, N: *How to talk back to your television set.* New York: Bantam Books, 1970).

8 Dominick, J R, and Rauch, G E: The image of women in network TV commercials. *Journal of broadcasting,* 16m 1972, pp 259–265.

9 Defleur, M L, and Defleur, L B: The relative contribution of television as a learning source for children's occupational knowledge. *American Sociological review,* 33, 1967, pp 777–789.

10 *BBC handbook 1975.* London: BBC, 1974.

11 Bogart, L: Warning: the Surgeon General has determined that TV violence is moderately dangerous to your child's mental health. *Public opinion quarterly,* 36, 1972–3, pp 491–521.

12 Biggs, J B: *Information and human learning.* Glenview, Illinois: Scott Foresman, 1971.

13 Schramm, W, Lyle, J, and Parker, E: *Television in the lives of our children.* Stanford, California: Stanford University Press, 1961.

14 Noble, G: Young children and television: some selected hypotheses and findings. *Screen,* 11, no 4/5, 1970, pp 31–47.

15 *Children as viewers and listeners.* London: BBC, 1974.

Chapter 3

THE EFFECTS OF EVERYDAY VIEWING

'Every generation is only twenty years away from <u>barbarism</u>. Twenty years is all we have to accomplish the task of civilizing the infants who are born into our midst each year.'

So writes Alberta Siegel, a professor of psychology at Stanford University. (1) She goes on to state that infants know nothing about communism, fascism, democracy, civil liberties, respect, decency, ethics, morality, conventions, and customs. Infants—'These savages', as she calls them—'know nothing of our language, our culture, our religion, our values or our customs of interpersonal relations'.

These young barbarians become mature adult people largely as a result of learning. They learn partly by trial and error, rewards and punishment contributing to the process. They develop attachments to adults, leading to desires to conform and meet adults' expectations. They learn through observing older people and imitating them. They also learn from oral instruction, and from graphic and pictorial representations. In short, human socialization proceeds via a variety of age-old learning situations and procedures, whereby the child uses his contacts with the environment to modify himself and to extend his powers in acceptable ways.

Modern man has been able to develop methods which bring about increased opportunities for learning. One such method is reading, which can be seen as providing a means of enormously enlarging the effective environment from which children may learn. Television is a more recent development, and one which reaches (or 'assaults') visual and auditory senses simultaneously. Very young children can learn from television; they do not first have to acquire a body of difficult skills, as is the case with reading. Nor does television demand the deliberate attention and conscious effort which are often necessary for reading. As Milton Shulman (2) has said, echoing Marshall McLuhan, the child *steps into* television, and is surrounded by it as if it were a warm bath. Television provides a version of all of life that is instantly available, in the child's home

50

and, as we have previously remarked, thousands of childhood hours are spent in its company. No wonder television is a powerful medium. For many children it is an ever-present part of the environment from which they gain those vital twenty years of experience which separate civilization from barbarism.

In this chapter we shall look at data on the effects of television and consider evidence concerning children's learning from the medium. There are both direct and indirect ways of attacking most problems. In seeking to discover how television influences children it is worthwhile to consider alternative kinds of information, each of which may cast some light upon the matter at hand. We have surveyed children's viewing habits and their perceptions of television contents, and the knowledge thus gained clearly contributes to our understanding of the medium's effects. Alternatively, it is possible to take a more direct approach, and undertake investigations that are explicitly designed to assess the effects of television. We shall now examine some findings of studies of this kind. As it happens, many of the researches that have been undertaken to measure the effects of television on children are specifically concerned with the impact of violent and aggressive contents. For the sake of convenience we shall consider the effects of televised violence in a separate chapter. Similarly, we shall also postpone to a later chapter consideration of those programmes deliberately designed to help children learn—Schools' Broadcasting in Britain and American programmes such as *Sesame Street,* for example. What remain for the present chapter are the non-violent 'informal' influences of every-day viewing.

The conceivable outcomes of watching television are numerous, but the majority of them fall into three broad categories. First, there may be effects upon a viewers's behaviour. New habits or skills may be gained, or the frequency of activities in a child's existing repertoire may alter. Secondly, a person's knowledge and interests may be affected as a result of what he has seen on television. Thirdly, the viewer's attitudes may be influenced. These three categories are by no means unrelated, and they are certainly not mutually exclusive. Attitudes are partly determined by knowledge, and both of these may influence an individual's actions.

Children's behaviour, attitudes and knowledge are each affected by many things, television being one among numerous influences. There is an inevitable element of artificiality in attempts to investigate the unique effects of one particular source of influence, be it television, housing, education, or the social services. What each of us knows and believes, and how he acts, are the outcome of a number of factors acting in combination.

51

Their joint impact is not simply the summation of their separate effects. In the present chapter we shall be citing evidence which shows that children and young people are affected in various ways by watching television. It is quite another thing to claim that the presence or absence in a child of a particular attribute, favourable or unfavourable, is due entirely to watching television, and there are extremely few circumstances in which such a claim might legitimately be made.

The enterprise of undertaking research into the effects of television is not lacking in practical difficulties. Things were easier for those investigators who carried out major studies in the 1950s, in the days before regular access to the medium became practically universal in advanced Western societies. At that time Schramm, Lyle and Parker (3) were able to compare children living in two Canadian towns which were broadly similar except that one received television transmissions and the other did not. In Britain Himmelweit, Oppenheim and Vince (4), working during the early fifties, were able to make straightforward comparisons between viewers and non-viewers at a time when television ownership was still far from universal. Nowadays, circumstances in which it is possible to make simple comparisons between viewers and non-viewers are sadly rare. R Brown has been able to capitalize upon the coming of television to a small isolated community in Northern Scotland (5), making a before-after comparison, and in 1971 details were published of an interesting proposed investigation in Darwin, Australia, where the advent of television was imminent. Unfortunately the project was cancelled for lack of funds. On the whole, investigations of television's effects that are based on comparisons between viewers and non-viewers are not often now feasible. The snag is that lack of access to television is usually associated with atypical conditions of isolation or poverty, or with abnormally unfavourable attitudes to the medium. These factors make it difficult to form matched comparison groups of viewers and non-viewers who are otherwise similar.

When comparisons between viewers and non-viewers are not feasible, it is necessary to make do with alternative research methods that are less than entirely satisfactory. The procedure adopted in many of the studies described in the previous chapter was to compare heavy viewers of television with individuals who watch less frequently. It is quite appropriate to do so if one simply intends to establish whether or not an association exists between television viewing and certain human characteristics. However, when one wishes to know if television *causes* a characteristic by which heavy and light viewers differ, it again becomes necessary

52

to 'match' the groups of viewers, that is, to ensure that they differ only in their viewing, and such matching is often virtually impossible. Fortunately, researchers have found ways of getting round some of the difficulties, and a number of effects of television can be investigated without requiring comparison studies.

Miscellaneous outcomes of viewing
Some of the facts discovered about television's effects refer to outcomes which do not fall neatly into any of the three categories, behaviour, knowledge and interests, and attitudes. For instance, in the early days of television there was considerable anxiety about the conceivably damaging influence of viewing upon eyesight, and experts gave all kinds of dire warnings. An article published as late as 1959 confidently recommends that the child should be seated directly in front of the screen at a distance six or seven times its width. The screen should be at eye level and no other light must fall upon it. The child must not eat while watching television; nor should he be put to bed until at least fifteen minutes after the end of the programme.

The fact of the matter is that no conclusive evidence of damage to eyesight has emerged. A Japanese study did show that viewing can temporarily reduce the eye's ability to adjust and focus, but the effect is temporary, and full recovery takes place within an hour. Undoubtedly, eyestrain can occur if viewing conditions are poor and if children sit very close to the set, but children who watch television do not suffer more frequently from eye complaints or headaches than those who view little or not at all. Some children with poor eyesight report strain and headaches after viewing, but the findings make it clear that the same amount of time spent in alternative activities involving concentrated visual perception—reading, for instance—would have similar effects. (4)

Sleep does not appear to be very markedly affected by watching television. British and American surveys agree in finding that children do go to bed later as an outcome of watching television, but on the average it only makes a difference of around fifteen minutes. (3, 4) Slightly higher figures were found in homes which had recently acquired television, but bedtime was not normally delayed by more than half an hour. As we have mentioned previously, a small number of young children do stay up very late watching television, and they tend to be children of low intelligence who can least well afford the loss of sleep. Some mothers have reported bedtime conflicts involving wrangling over viewing, but the facts show that television only becomes a focus for such conflicts in homes where bedtime problems occur in any case.

Many children dream about television. A recent American study found that about four out of ten six-year-olds do, and that the more they view the more likely they are to dream about the things seen on the box. (6) However, there is no evidence that children who view heavily dream more than other children. Furthermore, although about one child in four did agree with the statement that 'sometimes the things I see on television make me lie awake at night' viewers did not report more difficulties with sleeping than non-viewing children in a comparison group. (4)

Watching television sometimes leads to anxiety and fear. In the major study undertaken by Himmelweit and her colleagues, they attempted to find out what things frighten children, and to measure how television-induced fears vary according to age and sex. They tried, without much success, to discover general principles that would specify the kinds of programmes most likely to arouse fear. It was found that relatively stylized forms of violence, as in Westerns, for instance, were not often frightening to children aged seven and over. Fiction series that were less stereotyped in form than Westerns were more likely to prove frightening, if they contained elements of danger and violence.

Children differ considerably in what they are frightened by, and with young children it is especially difficult to predict which incidents will prove frightening. (4) Some young children are strongly upset by scenes of violence, but others are not bothered at all. Although eerie events and the strange, unfamiliar kinds of contents associated with horror series and science fiction tend to frighten children more than do incidents that take place within familiar formats, such as Westerns and other relatively stylized drama series, some events in very realistic programmes, especially those which involve children and domestic scenes, can be very frightening. My six-year-old daughter, who rarely bats an eyelid at televised horror and violence, was most distressed at a scene showing physical violence in a realistic family setting. It seems that violence which involves child-actors with whom a child viewer easily identifies may be very disturbing, especially when it takes place in domestic contexts.

Another kind of situation which is often frightening is that which brings to mind the child's own experiences of fear. Any parent knows that children can often be scared of darkness, especially in unfamiliar places or those where 'monsters' or 'robbers' might be lingering. A television programme depicting situations that are 'scary' in real life may cause fear in the young viewer. Incidents that a child can predict are

54

unlikely to be too frightening. However, it is worth emphasizing that what frightens one child may affect another child, albeit of the same age, quite differently. Familiarity with the medium is one important factor, children who watch television least being most frightened by what they see, although children who watch the most are more likely to dream about it.

Perhaps television companies ought to ban all programmes likely to frighten children. But in view of the wide range and variety of events that some children find frightening such a ban would be very difficult to implement, if not impossible. Like adults, most children enjoy being frightened up to a point, and it is unlikely that occasional experiences of fear have a powerful long-term influence, harmful or otherwise. The crucial question concerning the possibly frightening contents of television programmes is not whether or not children are frightened by what they see on television, but whether those who exhibit extreme and debilitating fearfulness report television programmes as being a major source of their fears. To my knowledge there is no real evidence on this matter.

Having dealt with some of the miscellaneous consequences of watching television, we can now turn to those outcomes which clearly relate to the viewer's behaviour and his activities. One consequence of television—perhaps not, strictly speaking, a direct effect, but an outcome of undoubted importance—is that the viewer does not engage in whatever alternative activities he would otherwise be following during the time spent in front of the screen. In the case of individuals who reached adulthood prior to the coming of television the medium may have led to the disruption or cessation of previous habitual activities. With children who have grown up in the television age it is possible that potentially valuable interests and activities may fail to emerge. What kinds of alternative activities are actually disrupted by television?

Television's influence on other activities

The early days of widespread television are associated with a rapid decline in cinema-going, to which the new rival medium undoubtedly contributed. As William Belson has made clear (7), by no means all the blame for the decline in British cinema attendances can fairly be laid on television. Cinema admissions rose consistently throughout World Way Two and reached a peak around 1947, following which there was a rapid decline until 1950. But at that date no more than ten per cent of homes had a television set, and the steepest decline occurred during a period of time when the number of regular television viewers was quite tiny. During the period 1950—

1955, on the other hand, over which the proportion of homes with television rose rapidly to two in five, the decline in cinema attendances was relatively slow, and the accelerated decline which took place in the late 1950s was not paralleled by any acceleration in the number of homes acquiring television sets. There was undoubtedly a relationship between the numerical rise in the one medium and the decline of the other, but Belson's figures make it clear that television was definitely not the sole cause of the large drop in cinema audiences.

What further kinds of activities are affected by television? Does it reduce the amount of time spent in entirely dissimilar ways, social life and hobbies, for example, or are the most-affected activities those which are similar to television in their form and function for the viewer, such as magazine and newspaper-reading? Does television most often take time from relatively trivial or 'time-filling' alternatives, or does it interfere with important parts of human life?

Among adult viewers, only during the first two or three years of television ownership is there any very marked disruption of prior life-styles. After roughly this period, the hobbies and previous habitual activities initially reduced by television tend to re-assert themselves, and the time taken up by viewing ceases to restrict viewers' pre-television major pursuits. This is true both for activities featured in television programmes, such as gardening, sports, and world events, and for those which tend not to be, such as playing darts, crossword puzzles and membership of clubs. For example, the amount of time devoted to gardening shows a sharp decline during the first year of ownership, but by the third year the average length of time spent gardening returns to its pre-television level.

In children, television takes time from alternative mass-media entertainments, including comic and magazine reading, but it does not greatly interfere with structured activities such as schoolwork and hobbies. (1) The introduction of television in Japan was associated with a reduction in time spent on homework and with diminished levels of reading ability, but this ill-effect has not been observed in Western countries. Apart from cinema-going and listening to the radio a number of additional activities are somewhat curtailed by television, but the magnitude of the impact on each of them is relatively slight. Bedtime is delayed a little, as we have previously remarked; reading-time is reduced, but the items affected are mainly comics and popular 'confession' and detective magazines and similar pulp materials. Accompanying the introduction of television there have been large initial drops in the numbers of books

56

read, but this appears to be a transitory phenomenon. (4) Radio is more seriously affected; not only does it receive less time—around half—than in the pre-television decades, but it has become a medium which individuals use mainly as a secondary activity, listening to the radio while doing something else, for instance, housework or driving.

It is virtually impossible to ascertain whether children brought up with television would distribute their time given to interests and activities in a markedly different manner were television non-existent. The data that have been made available from studies of the effects of the introduction of television suggest that for most children this is not so, the only activities that are markedly and permanently altered being those which are functionally similar—listening to the radio, going to the cinema, reading newspapers, comics and pulp magazines. The fact that watching television is chosen as the most-preferred activity only at times, such as after school, when children quite reasonably seek rest and relaxation rather than pursuits of a more active nature supports the assertion that the medium does not often interfere with the acquisition and practice of serious pursuits. However, lack of knowledge prevents our making any definite statement on this point. It is certainly possible that for some children the presence of a television in the home from early childhood onwards does inhibit the growth of useful skills and rewarding alternative activities.

Effects on children's behaviour

Most of those studies which have examined the direct effects of television contents on children's behaviour have concentrated on violent and aggressive kinds of acts, to be considered in the next chapter. In addition, there is some data, to be discussed later, concerning the effects on behaviour of programmes designed for young viewers. Some interesting facts emerge from an enquiry into the effects of American anti-smoking commercials. (8) Most of the participants were naturally adults, but a comparison between the effects upon older and younger people does reveal a striking contrast, making it clear that the young may be much more open than older individuals to certain kinds of behavioural change. The study took the form of a survey in which participants were asked whether they had seen anti-smoking commercials on television, and they were questioned about the effects of these programmes upon their own habits and attitudes. The participating sample of viewers was divided into two groups, 'young people under twenty-one' who attended high schools and a technical college, and 'the general population over twenty-one'. They were asked whether the advertisements had influenced their personal smoking habits, and about a third of both the students and the older respondents said they had cut down. A second question was less open to respondents' easy rationalizations and self-delusions in forming their replies. It asked whether the commercials had actually made them stop smoking, either permanently or temporarily. The response to this item indicated a very large difference between older and younger viewers in the programmes' influence on behaviour. A fifth of the students said they had stopped as a result of seeing the programmes, but none of the older people said the commercials had made them stop smoking. These findings strongly suggest that ventures which use the television medium to get across a message that will influence the audience's behaviour are much more likely to be successful with younger than with older viewers.

A number of claims have been made at one time or another for additional effects of television on children's behaviour, but in most cases there is an absence of unequivocal evidence. One suggestion is that television makes children passive, although what is meant by passive in this context is rarely made explicit. Insofar as a child can be said to possess a general trait of passivity, the evidence is that this is more likely to lead to heavy viewing rather than the reverse, and television may function as an 'electronic peer', being a convenient and undemanding companion for a passive child. (6)

Himmelweit and her colleagues have identified five distinct senses in which the term passivity has been used (4), and these authors found no clear evidence for television making children passive in any of them. First, they say, it is not true that child viewers are passive in the sense of absorbing television like a sponge. Nor is it true that television leads to children preferring an edited, televised, version of life to the real thing. Thirdly, as we have already noted, there is no evidence that as a result of viewing children become passive, in the sense of lacking initiative. A fourth possibility, that television leads to a jaded palate, appears to be contradicted by the evidence. In fact as a result of watching television many children become interested in a wider range of subjects and activities. Finally, there is no evidence that viewing dulls the imagination. No differences were found between viewers and non-viewers in a survey whereby teachers were asked to rate children along the dimension of imaginativeness.

Television does make children passive in one respect. While they are actually watching, boys and girls who may have been extremely active a few minutes previously are likely to become quieter and apparently more receptive. The contrast is especially marked in hyperactive children
58

such as some schizophrenic girls observed by one psychiatrist. (3) Normally these girls were noisy, unruly and frequently destructive, yet they would sit quietly watching television for hours. This observation has given rise to a number of psychiatric interpretations centring around the idea that television acts as a mother-substitute, satisfying infantile longings for someone to care, nurse and give comfort, and to provide warmth and constancy, steadily giving without ever demanding in return. It is reasoned that the children can have their infantile wishes and needs partially satisfied by the ever-available television set, and in consequence, passive and dependent oral character traits become fixed, if one continues to enjoy television. This is certainly an imaginative line of speculation, but not, in my opinion, any more firmly supported by hard facts than any of a number of alternative explanations of what was observed.

Another suggestion is that television causes children to withdraw from life. In considering this possibility one encounters once more some of the problems that plague efforts to confirm or deny the claim that the medium makes children passive. First, there is more than one kind of withdrawal. Secondly, even if we do find that a child who is prone to withdraw from certain aspects of life also devotes long hours to viewing, it would seem unlikely that television provides a main causal factor. Undoubtedly, a medium which makes few demands upon the viewer and which contains a fair measure of fantasy will appeal to a child whose personal relationships are unsatisfactory, just as a medium which contains much that is interesting and exciting will appeal to and be extensively used by a child who regards his own life as dull. But it is something else to state that watching television produces definite traits of character, and at present the available facts do not justify such an assertion.

A claim which cannot easily be either supported or dismissed is that television makes addicts of children. One difficulty is that addiction to television cannot so easily be defined as can, say, addiction to alcohol. In the case of the latter, levels of protracted drinking known to produce major physiological damage can be identified as tolerably clear indications of addiction. Except in the rarest instances, it is doubtful whether watching television can lead to serious physical harm. I have not encountered any cases of children who go without food or sleep in order that television may engage their continuous attention. It may be more realistic to equate television viewing in some children with the somewhat vaguely defined term 'mild addiction' that is sometimes used with reference to chemical stimulants including alcohol, tobacco and other drugs. An adult study has revealed phenomena not totally unlike withdrawal symptoms when

59

individuals volunteered to desist from viewing television, and were actually paid for not watching. (9) The experiment was carried out in Munich, West Germany, in 1971. Habitual viewers participated for a year, each couple receiving £4 per week for doing so. However, none of the one hundred and eighty-four individuals actually survived the year, all having returned to television within five months.

This demonstration of widespread reluctance to abstain from viewing suggests that many of us are heavily dependent upon television, but whether it indicates a harmful degree of addiction is open to question. It might be more legitimate to speak of addiction if viewers paid £400 per week, rather than £4, were equally unable to desist from viewing. But it is not likely that even the US government agencies who have happily thrown large amounts of cash into some television research ventures would be willing to support such an experiment.

As things are, hard facts about television addiction in children are practically non-existent. One social scientist has suggested that addiction may result when a child becomes accustomed to a heightened level of excitement. (3) If this level then declines he will be restless or bored. However, it is open to question whether the latter observation really proves anything except that children, like adults, tend to be displeased when things they are used to are taken away.

Does television influence the manner in which children play? It certainly provides play-contexts and play-heroes for younger children, just as it serves a 'coin-of-exchange' function in the conversation of adolescents. Half of the four-year-olds observed in one American study manifested some television influence in their normal play. (10) They imitated roles and actions portrayed in Westerns, cartoons and even the weather reports. It was observed that those kinds of play which involved television characters took on a stereotyped character. Whether television seriously influences the *kinds* of play in which boys and girls engage is open to question. The games children play remain surprisingly constant over the years, even if *Star Trek* and *Dr Who* may have largely replaced the cinema Westerns and thrillers that contributed heroes and villains for yesterday's play activities.

Many specific forms of behaviour are influenced by what we see on television, and some advertising companies might go out of business were this not the case. After the US comedy series by Rowan and Martin, *Laugh-In,* started using the expression 'Look that up in your Funk and Wagnalls' the company making the dictionary of that name had to increase its production by twenty per cent to satisfy the extra demand. (9)

The sight of the sprightly little Russian gymnast Olga Korbut sent thousands of British mums scurrying to enroll their daughters in local gym classes. Stock phrases and fads are regularly spawned by the medium. Producers of educational programmes in Denver and Los Angeles have capitalized upon the power of TV soap operas to influence viewers' behaviour. They have used the format with great success to communicate skills and knowledge important in jobs and health care to people living in ghetto areas.

Television and knowledge
When we turn from behavioural effects to consider the influences of television on children's knowledge and interests, we encounter a noticeable paucity of data to answer some of the most important questions that need to be raised. A certain amount of useful research has been undertaken, and it has contributed information concerning effects on vocabulary, general knowledge and on children's ranges of interest. Yet no serious attempt has been made to discover whether or not the long hours spent viewing really contribute in significant ways to children's conceptions of the world and to their understanding of their own lives. As we saw in the previous chapter, children believe the world that is depicted on television to be closer to real life than it actually is. This finding gives support to the suggestion that we really ought to know more than we currently do about television's contribution to young people's awareness and understanding of the way things are, especially in relation to those aspects of life that lie outside direct experience. According to the followers of Marshall McLuhan, television has brought about a fundamental revolution in our consciousness, transforming the world into a 'Global Village' in which awareness of and knowledge about people and events has been radically altered by the impact of the medium. McLuhan's claims may well contain a germ of truth, but the kind of scientific research that would inform us whether or not the coming of television has indeed contributed to marked changes in people's awareness of crucial aspects of life is still awaited. With television, are foreigners more or less foreign? Are we influenced more than we used to be by events in foreign countries, or by their manners, customs and fashions? Are we less parochial in our own habits and attitudes? Do we put more weight on international issues and their world-wide ramifications in forming our political attitudes and voting habits? Does increased exposure to people who follow a variety of religions influence our own beliefs? Do distances between places appear shorter as a result of regular transmission of television news items, and have physical distances become less important to

61

us? In what way does the depiction of contemporary wars on television, as in Vietnam or Belfast, influence our awareness of its effects on our attitudes to the combating sides? In short, is there a real meaning to the concept of a 'Television Age' whereby a medium is assumed to induce radically altered conceptions of the world in its viewers, and especially in the children who grow up with it?

At present, we frankly lack the facts that would make it possible to answer questions of this nature. The impressions of a journalist give some illumination, although they are no substitute for hard evidence. The journalist, Russell Baker, writing of rural Iowa at the time of the 1968 presidential election, observed that the people there seemed more pre-occupied with problems they had learned about through television than about practical issues affecting their prosperity and everyday lives. (1) He wrote, 'Other issues have become so overriding as to obscure the farmer's problems, even in his own mind. Through some miracle of modern communication and repetition, the farmer lives in rural solitude and dwells upon crime-filled city streets, fiery demonstrations, bloody riots, bearded campus protestors, the frustrating war in Vietnam.' Per-haps the coming of television has indeed made 'global villagers' of many of us, as this account suggests.

Some information is available about television's contribution to the informal acquisition of knowledge by children. Compared with adults children may learn either more or less from a particular programme. It is not easy to make broad generalizations about the amount which children can learn, since what is acquired is largely determined by the manner in which each individual perceives, interprets and understands what he sees and hears. In some instances, as we noted in the previous chapter, child-ren learn more about perceptual details than adults do. Findings of experimental research confirm this; children may be more successful than adults in remembering details of, say, the furnishing of a room or the clothes of a minor character. (1) But children do not remember more factual contents than adults. In one study it was found that eight-year-olds who watched films would subsequently recall sixty per cent of the facts recalled by adults. Doubtless the particular film contents influence the findings.

Television can enlarge the general vocabulary of your children. Six-year-olds who regularly watched television and whose general intelligence scores were either higher or lower than average were observed in one study to have a vocabulary level about one year more advanced than com-parable children who did not watch television. (4) But, for children of
62

average intelligence, no difference in vocabulary existed between viewers and non-viewers. The scientist who carried out this investigation also administered a 'Special vocabulary' test, made up of words such as 'Satellite', 'War' and 'Cancer' that were considered to be topical at the time (1959). Larger differences favouring viewers might have been expected with these items, but only in the case of the children of lower than average intelligence was there a difference of an order that could not easily have been due to chance.

A small number of studies have examined the impact of television on children's general knowledge. There is no doubt that television does provide opportunities for children to learn about all kinds of things, but whether they do so to any great extent depends largely upon what programmes the child actually watches. As we have remarked, the majority of child viewers use television primarily as a means of entertainment, and those who view most heavily tend to prefer programmes with an element of fantasy. Consequently, we would not expect to find that viewers necessarily acquire substantial amounts of general knowledge not possessed by non-viewers. Yet we might well find that individuals who choose to watch informative programmes gain more knowledge than either non-viewers of similar age and intelligence, or viewers who only watched entertainment programmes. Unfortunately, whilst research findings exist to supply information on queries of the former kind (ie, do viewers on the whole possess more knowledge than non-viewers) no data is available on the more detailed questions relating to the extent of non-educational television's effectiveness as a learning medium among children who choose to watch informative programmes.

Research in Britain has compared viewers and non-viewers aged ten to eleven and thirteen to fourteen for their knowledge of English literature, history, geography, science and religion. (4) Questions took the form of multiple-choice tests, in which the child ticked the correct answer from a number of alternative responses to a brief question (eg, 'What is the largest city?—Paris, Moscow, Berlin, New York')

The comparisons between viewers and non-viewers of various ages yielded very few significant differences. Among the younger children, viewers low in intelligence obtained higher scores for geography and science than comparable non-viewers; older middle-class boys (but not girls) who watched television and attended Secondary-Modern schools scored somewhat higher than non-viewers on a general test of knowledge of English Literature. But the mass of scores give the overall impression that, on the whole, general knowledge scores of viewers and non-viewers were roughly

63

equivalent, differences in particular sub-groups being equally balanced in favour of each. There were slight overall tendencies for younger, duller viewers to score higher than comparable non-viewers, and for brighter non-viewers to gain higher scores than brighter viewers, but the differences were not large and there were many exceptions.

The study that gave rise to the above findings was undertaken in the mid-fifties, and since that time there has been little satisfactory research into the possible effects of television on children's general knowledge. We do possess some information about the acquisition of some relatively specific forms of knowledge that are made available by television. Not surprisingly, it is found that heavy users of television know more than others about subject matter closely related to particular programme contents, including names of singers and information about the entertainment world—showbiz and pop. Surveys carried out in Japan have also demonstrated a positive relationship between heavy viewing and knowledge related to entertainment and sports. Furthermore, as remarked in the previous chapter, children who watch a good deal of television are better informed than others about certain occupational roles and their relative status in society, when these are often depicted on the screen.

Much of the incidental learning that takes place as children watch television relates to fads and trivia of little lasting importance. In the United States older students have played an amusing game called 'Trivia', made up of questions and answers about some of the ephemera made available via the mass media. The results give one indication of how effectively children can be taught during their childhood years. In a 'Trivia Contest' young adults paraded their childhoods' secretions of useless information, and answered such questions as 'Who was Bob Hope's radio announcer?', or 'Who was the singer of "Come on-a my House"?' Apparently the winner received a trophy for his success, which he credited to 'my garbage-filled mind', after listening to a chorus sing the Mr Trivia song, 'There he goes, think of all the crap he knows'. (1)

Watching television can undoubtedly affect a child's range of interests, since it exposes him to a variety of activities. It has been especially well used for presenting in an easily assimilated form areas of interest which might otherwise be restricted to particular minorities, such as the highly educated. The visual medium, combined with the personal approach of a teacher possessing flair and charm, can arouse widespread enthusiasm about a subject. Sir Mortimer Wheeler's programmes on archeology are a case in point; he was able to induce an awareness of the interest and importance of archeology to large numbers of viewers. More recently,

64

David Bellamy's series on botany, Ian Nairn's on the architectural environment, Jacob Bronowski's programmes on man and science and those of John Berger and Lord Clark, among others, provide further instances of successful attempts to put the resources of television to use for introducing people to new interests and unfamiliar aspects of civilization. But unfortunately we lack hard facts concerning the extent to which television has actually contributed to extending children's range of interests, or raised their levels of awareness, simply because the necessary research has yet to be undertaken.

The same conclusion must apply to questions about the effectiveness of television's role in illuminating social problems. Television has been arguably the most effective of all the mass media in making people aware of a wide range of human problems, ranging from pollution to homelessness. One observer considers it to have played an important role in changing people's reactions to psychological disorder, from ridicule or aversion into its acceptance as a form of illness that requires treatment and may be cured. (11) Yet once more we find that research findings to support or deny the contention that television has had the positive effect of making children more aware of social problems, are sadly lacking. There is no doubt that television does provide opportunities from which children may profit, but we simply do not know how many children actually do so, or by how much.

Before concluding this survey of the research into the effects of television upon children's knowledge and interests, patchy and in many respects unsatisfactory as it is, we can note that some studies have compared learning of peripheral items, such as articles of dress and physical scenery, with learning of central contents, such as the major themes or plots of a drama series. It was noted earlier that children sometimes remember perceptual details not recalled by adults. Memory for details such as the kind of clothing worn is more accurate in twelve-year-olds than in nine-year-olds, but thereafter declines slightly, girls scoring somewhat higher than boys at all ages. (12) Whereas learning of peripheral content increases up to early adolescence and then declines, learning of relevant central material continues to improve into young adulthood. It has been suggested that an outcome of presenting information via a visual medium is to provide more emphasis upon the central aspects of what is being presented, and less emphasis upon irrelevant and peripheral items, than occurs in a natural 'live' situation, but the results of an experiment carried out in order to test this hypothesis do not in fact support it. (13)

65

There are some differences in what is recalled following colour and black-and-white presentation. Colour facilitates recall of peripheral material, but in some circumstances individuals learn a greater number of central items following black-and-white visual inputs. (13) It is conceivable that the added realism which colour provides may interfere with learning of some central or thematic contents, directing individuals' attention to peripheral aspects of the presentation. One researcher claims that colour may alter the emotional impact of television: evidence consistent with this suggestion is contained in the reports of viewers who watched a funeral. Those who watched in colour indicated that they were more emotionally moved than viewers who saw the presentation in black-and-white. The non-colour viewers wrote longer and more detailed reports, however, and appear to have been more conscious of the commentators and sometimes irritated by them. Both of these findings were repeated in an experiment comparing black-and-white with colour versions of an American Football game. It is difficult to decide on an interpretation of this evidence, but it does appear that colour and black-and-white materials strike viewers differently. Perhaps the significance of the spoken word changes, and colour seems to make it possible for viewers to regard themselves less as observers and more as participants.

Effects of television upon attitudes
A number of investigations have been carried out to assess the possible effects of watching television upon attitudes. In adults, attitudes are relatively stable and not easy to alter. But children, by virtue of their naivity and immaturity, are less fixed in their opinions and beliefs, and hence less resistant to change.

The difficulty of changing adults' attitudes has been documented by investigations which measured the effects of viewing a number of British programmes that were expected to lead to attitudinal changes. Programmes studied were the BBC's *The Children of Revolution,* which was about the lives of young people in Czechoslovakia, *The Nature of Prejudice,* a seven-part Associated Television series, and *Rainbow City,* a six-episode BBC series on the lives of immigrants to the UK. (14) The programme on Czechoslovakia was successful in imparting knowledge about specific aspects of life in that country, but it did not bring about any change in general attitudes to Czechoslovakia as a political state. With the other items, the survey findings indicate that people saw what was uppermost in their own minds, rather than the points stressed by the programme,

66

and prejudiced viewers were noticeably successful in avoiding the anti-prejudice messages that the producers attempted to communicate. For instance, viewers of *Rainbow City* expressed considerable sympathy for the the particular characters portrayed, but this did not lead to any modification of viewers' attitudes to coloured people or to immigrants in general. It appears that identification or empathy with particular personalities does not necessarily stretch to the cultural or racial group in general.

In many respects it is fortunate that attitudes are so hard to change. A nation made up of individuals whose opinions can be altered willy-nilly by the efforts of politicians and advertisers to persuade people to change their minds and alter their habits would lack the element of stability that is essential in a healthy society. When attitudes do change, they tend to do so slowly and little-by-little. As Professor J D Halloran has written, 'We are not constantly poised on the edge of momentous decisions and fundamental changes, but we are continually making small adjustments and shifts in our position, by relating attitudes to behaviour in our day-to-day activities. Over a period of time these changes, barely perceptible at any given moment, may well accumulate and—in the final analysis—the many small adjustments or the constant chipping away may amount to something quite considerable.' (14)

In children, we might expect television to contribute to acquired attitudes, but practical and methodological problems make it more difficult to measure the effects of this one among many possible environmental influences upon attitude acquisition than to assess the power of the medium to change existing attitudes. Attitudes to authority among children may be influenced by the frequent portrayal of our leaders on television; we can see how they talk and behave while being grilled by Robin Day or chatted up by Joan Bakewell. Because of television, we may have cultivated, as Milton Shulman claims, 'a society that nightly obliterates with casual contempt the faces, the voices and arguments of its leaders'. (15) But one might also argue that our society at present is overly deferential, and inclined to forelock-tugging, and one in which attitudes to people in authority have been too respectful, too unquestioning. We ought to be suspicious of figures occupying high-status roles who want to be protected from the direct gaze of ordinary citizens.

Children's attitudes are more easily changed than those of adults. A study was undertaken some time ago to discover whether child attitudes towards a particular occupational group, taxi drivers, could be influenced by the image of them communicated in the mass media. (1) Six- and seven-year-olds heard a series of radio dramas in which the main character

67

was a taxi driver. Half the children listed to six episodes in which he got into some kind of trouble involving an argument or dispute with another person, and subsequently managed to get out of his difficulties by behaving towards the other individual in a violently aggressive manner. The other children listend to episodes that were identical to the first ones except for the ending. In these episodes the taxi driver was able to extricate himself by constructive, non-violent means. Later, the children were all shown a copy of the local newspaper, and those who demonstrated a reasonable understanding of the nature of press reports were questioned about the likely endings to some of the stories in the paper. First, each child was asked about some innocuous news items, concerning the weather and forthcoming school holidays, for instance. He then heard reports about taxi drivers, and was asked to finish the story. It was found that the endings the children supplied were strongly influenced by the endings to the programmes concerning taxi drivers they had heard on the radio. Most of the children who had listened to the radio series with the constructive endings finished the news item in a manner that involved no aggression on the part of the driver. However, when those who had heard the programmes in which taxi drivers had acted violently were asked to complete the report about a local driver in a real problem situation, half of them reported highly violent actions by the taxi driver, and only a third finished the story in a way which involved no aggression at all.

Findings such as these do not provide conclusive proof that attitudes as such can easily be changed, but they do indicate the possibility of change. Research undertaken in the 1930s to examine the effects of certain films on children's attitudes provides further evidence of altered attitudes. Children aged between seven and twelve each saw up to three feature films from a list which included *Birth of a Nation*, which has scenes showing black Americans in a markedly unfavourable light, *All Quiet on the Western Front* (a strongly anti-war film) and *Journeys End*. (16) Some attitudes changed after seeing the film. For instance, attitudes towards war became more negative, and attitudes towards Chinese and German people became more positive. Watching *Birth of a Nation* led to persisting unfavourable attitude changes towards negroes. In general, attitudes altered in the direction of those implicit in the films that were shown, and bigger changes took place in children who watched two or three of the films than in those who saw only one.

One of the few attempts made to investigate the effects of television as such on young people's attitudes was based upon a US programme

68

called *The National Citizenship Test.* (17) This contained a number of short dramatic scenes demonstrating activities which the United States Constitution specifies as being either legal or illegal. Typical scenes portrayed a speaker criticizing the government and a policeman entering a suspect's home. After each sequence the audience was told to consider the legality of the actions depicted, and a description of the constitutional law covering these actions was presented. A questionnaire including items testing attitudes was distributed to high school students before and after the programme was seen, the distribution of the tests to some students who did not see the programmes providing a necessary control. The results showed that the programmes did influence attitudes. The authors are vague about the precise nature of the changes, the attitude scale being described as containing opinion items based on constitutional laws similar but not identical to those discussed in the programme. Students who saw the programmes subsequently agreed with these items more often than others.

Taken as a whole, the evidence indicates that television can and does influence children's attitudes. Indeed it would be surprising if this were not the case, in view of children's vulnerability and naivity with respect to television contents and their noticeable willingness to believe in the true-to-life nature of what they see on the screen. It is difficult to say whether or not regularly watching television makes children more tolerant or more aware than they would otherwise be. It depends partly on what they watch, and partly upon what they would be doing with the time if not watching television. We do know that some programmes have strongly affected many people. The attitudes and feelings which *Cathy Come Home* or *Edna the Inebriate Woman* or *Johnny Go Home* (granted that audiences are to some extent self-selecting) may well be large, but while appropriate research is lacking we simply do not know. Finally, we ought not to overlook the conceivable influence upon both children's and adults' attitudes of some programmes ostensibly designed for and largely watched as straightforward entertainment. The possible effects of, say, Tony Hancock's television series, or *Steptoe and Son* merit examination. Discussing *Till Death Do Us Part*, Peter Black writes that its author, Johnny Speight, has been 'letting the healing light of laughter into some dark corners of human prejudice'. (18) What a marvellous achievement, if it can be realized!

REFERENCES
1 Siegel, A: The effects of media violence on social learning. Pp 613-636 in Schramm, W, and Roberts, D F (eds): *The process and effects of mass communication.* Revised edition. Urbana, Illinois: University of Chicago Press, 1971.

2 Shulman, M: *The least worse television in the world.* London: Barrie and Jenkins, 1973.

3 Schramm, W, Lyle, J, and Parker, E: *Television in the lives of our children.* Stanford, California: University of California Press, 1961.

4 Himmelweit, H T, Oppenheim, A N, and Vince, P: *Television and the child.* London: Oxford University Press, 1958.

5 Brown, J R, Cramond, J K, and Wilde, R J: *Children and television: second progress report.* Mimeographed report, Centre for Television Research, University of Leeds.

6 Bogart, L: Warning: the Surgeon General has determined that TV violence is moderately dangerous to your child's mental health. *Public opinion quarterly,* 36, 1972–3, pp 491–521.

7 Belson, W A: *The impact of television: methods and findings in program research.* London: Crosby Lockwood and Son, 1967.

8 O'Keefe, M T: The anti-smoking commercials: a study of television's impact on behaviour. *Public opinion quarterly,* 35, 1971, pp 242–248.

9 Johnson, N: *How to talk back to your television set.* New York: Bantam Books, 1970.

10 Noble, G: Young children and television: some selected hypotheses and findings. *Screen,* no. 4/5, 1970, pp 31-47.

11 Bogart, L: Social sciences and the mass media. In Yu, F T C (ed): *Behavioral sciences and the mass media.* New York: Russell Sage Foundation, 1968.

12 Hale, G A, Miller, L K, and Stevenson, H W: Incidental learning of film content: a developmental study. *Child development,* 39, 1968, pp 69–77.

13 Abel, J D, and Kramer, F: Incidental learning from television: an overview. Mimeographed article, Michigan State University.

14 Halloran, J D: The social effects of television. Pp 25–68 in Halloran, J D (ed): *The effects of television.* London: Panther Books, 1970.

15 Shulman, M: *The ravenous eye.* London: Cassell, 1973.

16 Leifer, A D, Gordon, N J, and Graves, S B: Children's television: more than entertainment. *Harvard educational review,* 44, 1974, pp 213–245.

17 Alper, S W and Leidy, T R: The impact of information transmission through television. *Public opinion quarterly,* 33m 1969, pp 556–562.

18 Black, P: *The biggest aspidistra in the world.* London, BBC, 1972.

Chapter 4

CHILDREN AND TELEVISION VIOLENCE

A report appeared recently in my local newspaper, the Exeter 'Express and Echo', under the headline GANG COPIES A TELEVISION IDEA ON A BURGLARY. Apparently the burglars used a method of cutting window glass they had seen on the television series *Dixon of Dock Green*. They received prison sentences of up to three years, and one of them asked for sixty-five other offences to be taken into consideration. The judge commented that their crimes provided 'yet another example to television producers of the undesirability of exhibiting methods of committing crime'.

The mass media have long provided convenient scapegoats for the most glaring of society's ills, and the visual communication systems have been especially popular as objects of blame. As early as 1916 a Parisian gentleman drew up an indictment of the cinema, which he claimed was a 'propagator of vice and crime', and over the years both cinema and television have frequently been charged with providing the breeding grounds for all kinds of social disturbance.

Numerous horror-stories have been cited in the press and elsewhere, bearing witness to the apparently evil effects of the television medium. The book produced in 1961 to describe the major survey by Schramm, Lyle and Parker, reported a number of such tales. One described the arrest of a sixteen-year-old boy who had been seen entering the cellar of a house. The boy was wearing gloves, and he claimed that he had learned to do so from television shows he had seen, in order not to leave fingerprints. Another account concerned a boy aged nine. After showing his father a highly critical school report card the boy proposed improving the situation by giving the teacher a Christmas present in the form of a box of poisoned sweets. He explained that this technique had been demonstrated on the previous week's television, being used by a man who had decided to kill his wife. A third child, aged seven, was observed to be sprinkling ground glass into the lamb stew which formed the family

71

meal. Apparently he was simply curious to know if it really would work as it did on television.

Such stories are by no means uncommon. Whether or not they amount to real evidence that television has caused children to indulge in anti-social behaviour, as well as influencing the form of anti-social acts, the manner in which they are typically reported in the press indicates a strong belief that television is to blame. It would be absurd to deny that television does provide children and adults with information and ideas that can affect the form and content of activities of an anti-social or criminal nature. Any medium by which information about the world is communicated can have this function. Each James Bond book provides instances of inspiration for illegal activities. This is no new phenomenon; the pre-war writings of authors such as Edgar Wallace, 'Sapper' and Sax Rohmer, whose books sold in hundreds of thousands, are full of highly violent and sadistic incidents. In these books the psychopathic bully-boy British heroes set horrific examples to their readers, as they dealt with the Dirty Italians, Dago's and other Foreigners, and the Jewboys, Niggers and the snarling Opium-Smoking Orientals who held a constant and inexpressibly evil threat to Western Civilization. Anyone who complains of prejudice or xenophobia in today's heroes, or who is offended by their use of violence and alternative means of dubious morality in order to achieve their ends, can take a modicum of comfort from the fact that standards of conduct in today's thrillers are no lower than they were in the past.

Yet television is an especially powerful and widely accessible medium. Its introduction in several countries has coincided with rises in crime rates and in other indices of social disruption. Milton Shulman (2) has claimed that the years 1964 to 1968, during which the 'first telly generation the world had ever seen moved into adolescence and delinquency', happened also to be a period during which social trends in Britain and America began to heighten and intensify in an abnormal manner. These, he claims, took the form of an increase in juvenile violence, together with 'a blossoming of the hippie movement with its rejection of conventional morals and standards, an unprecedented revulsion against parental and establishment authority, a startling rise in drug-taking, a standstill in reading standards and a diminution of interest in literacy'.

Do the contents of such remarks add up to a case against television? One problem is deciding whether or not the incidence of anti-social activities over this period really sets it apart from previous years. These phenomena might simply be manifestations of trends which had been

72

developing over a long period. Also, even if we accept that these years did witness an intensification of certain anti-social actions, their co-occurrence with the coming to maturity of the first 'telly generation' might be coincidental. Thirdly, it is quite likely that a large number of positive social changes during the same period would equally easily be identified, or the intensification of positive trends. Fourthly, the suggestion that television leads to revulsion against parental authority, whether we consider such a trend to be undesirable or benign, appears to be contradicted by other evidence. A survey investigation described in the previous chapter (1) showed that heavy viewing during adolescence is associated, in America at least, with high levels of conventionality and with political conservatism, and is negatively correlated with rejection of authority and parental morals. Fifthly, the years which saw the introduction of television were also ones in which a number of other potentially potent social, economic and educational changes occurred, so it would be difficult to assess the unique contribution of television. As we have already pointed out most social changes are caused by numerous factors, among which television is but one.

The real problem with trying to assess the validity of broad claims about the effects of television such as those raised by Mr Shulman is that too many separate factors are involved for objective and adequately controlled investigation to be feasible. The limitations of scientific resources and procedures force us to be more analytic in our approach, to ask questions that have greater precision and are somewhat narrower, in order to identify the real effects of television. Mr Shulman may well be largely correct in inferring that television does contribute to the broadly based social changes he has identified, but to discover if he is right we have to undertake investigations that consider more detailed kinds of evidence, and, at least initially, to concentrate our attention on those possible causes and effects that can be readily measured and, if possible, manipulated in controlled scientific research.

Some kinds of evidence are sufficiently compelling to demonstrate television's influence even in the absence of scientific measurement and control procedures. For example, Alberta Siegel (3) has described the events in 1966 following presentation on American television of a film called *The Doomsday Flight,* in which a bomb is placed in an airliner by a mentally deranged individual. He subsequently keeps teasing the airline officials with pieces of information about his arrangements for exploding the bomb. When the film was shown one bomb threat was telephoned to a US airline whilst it was still on the air. Another four were received during the following day. Eight more reached various airlines in the United States during the following week. The total number of threats, all of which were fortunately hoaxes, was at least four times that normally received over a similar period.

The amount of research to which our understandable preoccupation with the effects of television violence has given rise is quite considerable. In considering evidence about effects of violence we are happily free from the necessity to undertake some of the barrel scraping that was necessary to find facts relevant to questions we wished to raise about other effects of the medium. The relative wealth of data about the outcomes of television violence enables us to be selective and to concentrate on well-designed investigations that have been undertaken fairly recently. I have not attempted to provide an exhaustive survey of the hundreds of published studies of television violence.

Prior to examining evidence we need to decide what kinds of possible effects of television violence to look for. Our main concern is with effects that have clear social implications, and a bearing upon the manifestation of violence, delinquency and aggression in the individual viewer. Four possible effects can easily be identified. These are neither exhaustive nor mutually exclusive, but taken together they do represent some of the most probable effects upon people, and one which can readily be measured.

The first effect is to influence the viewer's behaviour. The suggestion is that watching a television programme containing violence may cause a child to perform violent or aggressive actions. These might be acts which are novel to the viewer, in which case he might be regarded as learning a new response from the medium, observing and later imitating what he sees there. Alternatively the acts might already be familiar to him, the main effect of seeing them on television being to encourage their use, or to remind the viewer of them, or to perform the function of 'disinhibiting' him from performing acts which he otherwise would have kept in check.

A second way in which violence on television might influence the viewer is by increasing his tolerance of violence in others. Thus a child who has recently watched a violent programme, or an individual who has regularly seen violent contents over a long period of time, might be less inclined than others to attempt to prevent other individuals behaving in a violent or aggressive manner, or to discourage them from violent actions.

Related to this effect is a third possibility, that children's attitudes to the use of violence in general may be influenced as a result of being

74

exposed to violent television. For instance, it is conceivable that frequent exposure to drama series in which characters commonly attempt to deal with their frustrations and problems by acting aggressively may encourage a viewer to believe that violent ways of getting things done are legitimate or likely to succeed, or both. If a child comes to believe that acting violently is the normal way of dealing with a range of problems, and at the same time learns *how* to act violently from watching violent situations on television (or in real life, for that matter), he will be more likely to acquire violent habits than an individual whose exposure to violence is comparatively limited. The high incidence of violent behaviour among children in Belfast, and the high likelihood of baby-battering by parents who were themselves battered as children, provide compelling illustrations of the importance of social learning through the observation and imitation of others. There is little doubt that watching television, as well as 'real life', can bring about such learning in young children. This is especially probable among children who believe that what they see on television is largely true-to-life.

The fourth possible outcome of television violence is that children's sensitivity to violence may be altered. The suggestion is that one's perception of violent acts may be 'blunted' by prolonged exposure, viewers becoming less likely to notice or to be aware of violent acts that have been committed.

Alternative research methods

There is more than one way to assess the effects of television violence. One research method uses surveys as the means of investigation. Another approach is to undertake laboratory experiments. A third is to use 'field experiments'. These three approaches are each relatively distinct, although the borderlines between them are somewhat blurred. Survey methods and laboratory approaches each have characteristic advantages and limitations. Researchers who undertake field experiments typically attempt to design studies that combine the advantages of both surveys and experiments, but it is not always easy to do so without also incurring some of their disadvantages.

Survey methods were used for most of the investigations described in previous chapters. Broadly speaking, survey techniques attempt to assess or measure what people do, think, believe or know, but without artificially manipulating or influencing them in any way. Survey methods often provide a good means of detecting whether phenomena tend to occur together. Thus, if we want to find out if children who eat lots of chocolate are more intelligent than children who eat no chocolate, or whether babies

75

born in April are bigger than babies born in May, survey methods are likely to be suitable. If we want to discover if children who watch a good deal of television are more aggressive than others we might use a survey to do this, possibly comparing viewers and non-viewers on an agreed measure of aggression, or, if this is not possible, comparing heavy viewers and light viewers.

The survey is normally the method preferred by sociologists. A major advantage of survey techniques is that they usually enable observations to be based upon how individuals act in natural circumstances. It is not necessary to manipulate subjects or to place them in artificial situations. An advantageous feature of much of the data obtained from surveys is that it is likely to refer to relatively stable viewer characteristics. But this is not always the case, nor is it inevitably true that the findings of alternative methods merely indicate short-term changes.

A disadvantage of survey methods is that their conclusions are generally restricted to statements about associations or correlations between phenomena. A survey may tell us that there exists a relationship between observed violence in children and heavy viewing of violent programmes. What we would often like to know is whether one observed factor *causes* another. For instance, does watching many violent television programmes lead a child to behave aggressively? Simply demonstrating that there is a relationship between the two does not justify our assuming that a cause-and-effect relationship exists. It is quite possible that the aggressive behaviour is caused by a third factor, or group of factors, which happen, for any of a number of possible reasons, to be related to both of the variables measured in the survey.

Although the correlational kinds of evidence that surveys yield can never provide clear proof of a cause-and-effect relationship, they can sometimes give a strong indication that one exists, and survey designers have demonstrated considerable ingenuity in using surveys to discover possible causes. By way of illustration, if we were to find that heavy viewing was strongly associated with violent behaviour in the viewer, and that the relationship between the two was much stronger than the relationship between violence and all of the conceivably related additional factors we could imagine, we might be justified in saying that the evidence indicated a considerable likelihood that one of these two variables did influence the other. In some instances a further indication of possible causal factors can be obtained from correlational survey evidence when temporal factors are taken into account. Thus, if heavy viewing in January is associated with violent behaviour in February but there is no correlation
76

between heavy viewing in February and violent behaviour in January, we might interpret the pattern of observed relationships as suggesting that heavy viewing may lead to violent behaviour, but not *vice versa*.

Laboratory experiments in the social sciences are most often undertaken by psychologists, although psychologists do also sometimes carry out surveys, and sociologists occasionally perform experiments. Likewise, sociologists tend to measure respondents' attitudes, knowledge and opinions and to make use of available data on behaviour, such as delinquency records and crime reports, whilst psychologists are, generally speaking, more likely to measure physical behaviour. The overriding advantage of experiments is that they provide a means of exerting close control over the factors of interest to the scientist. Working in his own laboratory, the experimental psychologist is able to create a carefully controlled environment into which various elements can be introduced and varied at will, and their effects measured. Thus, an experiment undertaken to measure the effects of exposure to violence might contain two groups of human subjects who are as alike as possible in every respect except that one group is exposed to violence and the other is not. If the individuals who witness violent events subsequently act in a manner which is substantially different from the other subjects it is reasonable to conclude that exposure to violence probably caused or instigated the behaviour. By systematically manipulating a number of variables, and examining the effects of single factors or combinations of them, the psychologist is able, at least in theory, to demonstrate how children's behaviour is influenced by any number of environmental events.

A major disadvantage of experimental methods is that in the process of achieving the necessary degree of control for a valid experiment, the investigator is likely to produce a situation which is in some respects artificial and unlike the circumstances of everyday life. However, there are various ways of minimizing the artificiality of experimental situations, and with child subjects it is sometimes possible to disguise from them many if not all of the artificial aspects of an experimental situation.

On the whole, the tight control of events that is possible with experimental research makes experimental methods ideal for ascertaining whether or not certain factors *can* influence children. Their artificiality has the effect of making experiments generally less appropriate for considering questions relating to whether the same factors actually *do* regularly influence the same children in real life. In addition to any artificiality of experiments that resides in their 'unreal' nature—as a function of their non-natural laboratory contexts, the mere fact that one is manipulating one factor at a time, or at most a small number, provides an element of unreality, since in everyday life people's attitudes and actions are probably determined by a large number of influences. For reasons of this kind doubts have been expressed about the applicability of the analytical methods customary in the 'traditional' physical sciences such as physics and chemistry, in which relatively distinct cause-and-event sequences can be identified, to the complex circumstances of human life, where multiple determination is the rule.

Experimental field studies, which attempt to combine the naturalistic approach of survey methods with the controlled circumstances of experimental investigations, can be undertaken only when conditions permit. The experimenter cannot always choose the timing of and duration of his study; typically he has to take advantage of a 'ready made' natural situation involving some change that permits a controlled comparison. The situations observed in field studies are normally ones in which other social agencies, for example, schools, hospitals, social welfare departments are also closely involved, and their needs can often be at variance with those of the researcher. Having to fit in with the needs and requirements of others sometimes results in compromises which lessen the adequacy of the research design. We shall see one such instance in a field experiment that is described later.

Evidence from surveys

Some of the earlier major survey investigations that attempted to assess the effects of television violence formed parts of the large scale studies undertaken by Himmelweit, Oppenheim and Vince in Britain (4), and by Schramm, Lyle and Parker in North America (5). The findings of Himmelweit and her colleagues with respect to aggression were inconclusive. When teachers rated the aggressiveness of their children, no differences between viewers and non-viewers emerged. It was concluded that television is unlikely to cause aggressive behaviour, although it might precipitate aggression in emotionally disturbed individuals. However, these authors did not find that viewing violence and crime had the effect of discharging aggressive findings, as some writers had claimed, and it was noted that many of the mothers who had been asked to keep diaries describing their child's viewing habits did mention instances of aggressive play after a child had been watching Westerns on television.

The study by Schramm, Lyle and Parker yielded firmer evidence of a relationship between viewing and child aggression. Among children in the United States there was more expression of attitudes favouring anti-

78

social aggression by those who were heavy users of television than by those who had little contact with the medium. The difference was statistically significant in older children but not among ten-year-olds, and a different finding emerged from investigations undertaken in Canada. There it was found that twelve-year-olds who watched television were actually less aggressive than those who did not.

In surveys undertaken more recently closer attention has been paid to the manner in which aggression is measured, and there has been greater stress upon careful examination of the effects of violence. In the two earlier general studies of the medium violence formed but one among a large number of areas of interest. A further limitation of the data on effects of violence obtained from the early studies lies in the fact that in neither of them was there a direct measure of the actual amount of television violence seen by the children.

A number of recent survey-based investigations formed part of United States Government inquiries into violence and its effects in the mass media. In one study carried out during 1970 (6) the investigators examined the viewing habits of a sample of about four hundred American boys aged nine to twelve. The amount of violence watched by each boy was measured, and the boys were also rated for their beliefs in the effectiveness of violent means of solving conflicts, their willingness to use it themselves to deal with problems, their approval of violence in others, and their tendency to suggest violent methods of solving problems. These were assessed by asking the child to state his agreement or disagreement with statements such as 'A fight is the best way to settle an argument once and for all' (effectiveness); 'Anybody who says bad things about me is looking for a fight' (willingness); 'It's all right if a man slaps his wife' (approval); or to show how he would solve a problem, for example, 'Pretend somebody you know takes something away from you and breaks it on purpose. What would you do?' (suggestions).

It was found that the greater the quantity of television violence to which a boy was exposed, the more likely he was to express a willingness to resort to violence himself, to consider violence to be effective and to suggest violent solutions to problems. Thus, heavy consumers of television violence were more heavily rated in all of the attitudinal components except that relating to approval of aggression. Very similar findings were obtained in a follow-up study carried out in London during 1972 on British children. (1) Again, the greater the amount of violent content seen the more willing a child was to use violence himself and regarded violent solutions as being more effective. Slightly less aggressive attitudes

79

were observed in the older children, boys being more aggressive than girls. But relationships between aggressive attitudes and television exposure to violence were found among children of all ages, irrespective of social class and race. Correlations were also calculated to determine whether viewing of non-violent television programmes was also related to attitudes towards aggression. Some positive correlations did emerge from this analysis, but most of these were appreciably lower than the correlations between aggressive attitudes and exposure to television violence.

An interesting finding was that the relationship between aggressive attitudes and the amount of violence seen was affected by the kind of programmes in which the violence occurred. Thus watching Westerns was not related to aggressive attitudes, but watching other kinds of violent programmes was related. It is suggested by the authors that quite early in their viewing careers children are able to discount the violence attending the 'historical fantasy' of Westerns, whereas violent content in contemporary programmes is harder to deal with, and perhaps more likely to influence the child. The authors point out that while this study supports other evidence in showing that there is indeed a relationship between children's aggressive attitudes and a tendency to watch programmes high in aggressive themes, this relationship is a moderate one. We definitely cannot attribute a childs' aggression solely to the watching of television violence.

Aggression appears to be similarly unrelated to boys' preferences for the kinds of violent action found in contact sports such as ice-hockey, American football, boxing and wrestling. (8) On the other hand, amongst girls, ratings of aggression by the participants themselves and by their peers were positively related to a liking for these violent sports.

In one study carried out in the United States more than two thousand adolescents were asked to list their four favourite television series. These reports were transformed into violence measures, using a violence rating for each programme. Next, correlations were calculated between these scores and each of a number of measures of antisocial attributes. These included scores for aggressive and violent acts, such as getting into fights and hurting others, petty delinquency, and defiance of parents. It was found that the greater the violence ratings of a child's favourite programmes, the higher the score for anti-social activities. Furthermore, those young people who preferred to watch violent programmes were the most likely to approve of the use of violence, confirming the findings of previous investigations.

80

The relationship between aggressive behaviour and preference for violent television programmes is also documented in another large-scale study of American adolescents. (6) Individuals who listed violent series among their favourite shows were fifty per cent more likely to have been involved in serious fights at school or at work than individuals who did not include any violent programmes in their list of favourites. Similarly, those who preferred violent programmes were much more likely to have hurt some other person badly enough to require bandages or the services of a doctor, to have hit one of their teachers or supervisors, or to have taken part in gang fights and to have used a knife or gun as a weapon in order to get something from another person. They also reported more thefts, arson and trouble with the police.

The findings of the above studies and those of a number of additional survey investigations make it clear that relationships do exist between the expression of aggression in children and adolescents and their viewing on television of programmes that incorporate large amounts of violence. But, as we have already remarked, studies of this kind do have limitations, an important one being that their findings tell us virtually nothing about matters of cause and effect. They indicate that the viewing of violence and the expression of aggression in attitudes and behaviour are related, but they give little indication as to whether watching violent content can cause aggression. As I have said, survey methods are not, on the whole, particularly good for elucidating causal links, but data from surveys can sometimes yield information about the likelihood of such links, as the following instances show. We mentioned that there are two kinds of techniques which make it possible to infer from survey data that one of two related measures is likely to have contributed as a causal factor, leading to the other. First, to expand our previous reasoning, when we find that factor A and factor B are related, and that the positive correlation between A and B is larger than the correlation between A and all the other factors known to be related to it, and larger than that between B and all the other related factors, we can suppose that the link between A and B is a relatively direct one, and possibly causal in nature.

Secondly, we are given a hint of a possible causal linkage and an indication of its direction if we find that these exist and a substantial positive correlation between factor A on one occasion and factor B on a later occasion, but that the correlation between factor B on the first occasion and factor A on the later occasion is small or negative. The month-by-month television violence and child aggression example given above provides one illustration. By way of a second example, research into child development shows that there is a larger correlation between a mother's behaviour to the child in the earliest months of life and the child's crying in the subsequent period than between the child's behaviour in the earliest period and the mother's subsequent behaviour. This observation indicates a likelihood that the observed relationship between maternal behaviour and infant crying is due to the child's crying having been influenced by the mother's behaviour. In the absence of the temporal analysis, the simple correlation could equally easily have been explained by the suggestion that the child's crying influenced the mother's behaviour (and in fact this may also happen, to some extent).

This more detailed kind of analysis was used with the findings of a recent American survey investigation. (6) Six hundred adolescents answered questions about their viewing habits, their reactions to violence on television and their own behaviour. As in some other survey studies, they were asked to report on which programmes they watched from a list of popular series which had been rated for amount of violent content. These responses were used to assign a measure of violence-viewing to each of the participants. Data concerning aggression obtained from the self-reports was augmented by information from each respondent's teacher, his peers and his mother. For instance, mothers were asked how the child would act in an argument, and how the amount of fighting in which he was involved compared with that of other adolescents. The questions answered by the respondents themselves included items concerning their probable responses to imaginary conflict situations, a list of statements to which the respondent had to express his agreement or disagreement (eg, 'When I lose my temper at someone, once in a while I actually hit him') and a rating of actual delinquent and aggressively anti-social past behaviour. In sum, a fairly comprehensive aggregate of measures of aggression was obtained for each of the participating adolescents.

As in the other surveys, the findings of this one showed the viewing of violent contents to be related to aggression, as rated both by the self-reports and by the ratings of mothers, peers and teachers. One finding was that the correlation between aggression at present and seeing violence on television in the past was larger than the correlation between aggression and present viewing of television violence. This result is consistent with the suggestion that over a period of time exposure to violence on television does lead to the acquisition of aggressive activities.

A number of additional factors were found to be related to the amount of television violence that was seen. These included parental actions in controlling exposure to violence on television, forms of punishment at home, patterns of communication within the family and social class. A statistical technique known as 'Partial correlation' was used to determine whether any of these contributed substantially to the observed relationship between aggression and exposure to violence. This makes it possible to 'subtract' the contribution made by additional related factors to the correlation between the two variables of major concern, in this case, television violence and respondents' aggression. After doing so, if the positive correlation between the two variables remains equally large, or almost so, we can deduce that the additional factors do not make a substantial contribution to the relationship.

The investigators used partial correlation techniques to subtract out the effects of social class, school performance, total viewing time, forms of parental punishment, and parental affection. After removing all these possible sources of influence a statistically significant positive correlation between seeing violent programmes and being aggressive remained. Subtracting some of the sources of possible influence did not alter the correlation at all, but the elimination of others slightly reduced it. Analyses based upon data from others' reports of aggression produced very similar findings to those of the self-reports. These results led the investigators to conclude that regardless of viewing time, socioeconomic status and school performance, adolescents who have watched considerable amounts of violence on television tend to have acquired high levels of aggressive behaviour.

Among the many survey investigations that have been undertaken, the one which on its own makes the most convincing case for the hypothesis that watching violent television does lead to aggression in children is a study undertaken in two stages separated by ten years. (9) The research team was headed by Dr Leonard Eron. The first stage involved 875 nine-year-old children. Their aggression was assessed by a technique in which each child in a class rated all the other children on measures of physical and verbal aggression. This yielded a score for each child, based on the combined assessments of all the other children in his class. To assess the amount of television violence each child watched his mother was asked about the programmes he saw. As in the majority of survey investigations into television violence there was a relationship between aggression and the viewing of violence. Boys who saw a great deal of violent action on television tended to be more aggressive than the others. However, there was no such relationship among the girls.

The second stage of this investigation was carried out ten years later, at which time the investigators were able to locate slightly over half of the original participants. By now they were nineteen years of age. Once more, measures of both aggression and of exposure to violent television programmes were obtained. At this point the investigators used statistical procedures to calculate the degree of association between the scores of aggression and violence seen on television at the two widely separated times.

Their reasoning went like this. If there is a causal link between watching violent television and aggression, one would expect to find a positive correlation between the amount of violence seen at age nine and the degree of aggression exhibited at a subsequent time, as measured ten years later in the second stage of the study. In fact these are positively correlated ($r = +.3$) for the boys, although not for the girls. So far so good, but this correlation, alone, does not prove that seeing violence leads later aggression. However, some further evidence strengthens the case for a cause-and-effect relationship. Another calculation was carried out to measure the correlation between aggressive behaviour at age nine and violence watched on television ten years later. If it really is true that television leads to later aggression, and that the correlation between the two measures is due to such a causal link, we would expect the correlation between aggression at age nine and the viewing of television violence at nineteen to be small or non-existent. On the other hand, if the correlation between violence seen by nine-year-olds and aggression at nineteen is due not to a causal connection but to some other factors, we would expect to find an equally strong relationship between the latter two measures, aggression at age nine and viewing at nineteen. The degree of association between these scores happens to be nil, that is, there is no significant correlation ($r = .01$) between them.

This chain of thought may be difficult to follow, but it points rather convincingly to the likelihood that the preference for watching violent television contributes to the development of aggressive habits. The patterns of observed correlations are hard to reconcile with alternative explanations especially since the correlations between aggression and television violence at each of the two ages ($r = .21$ at age nine; $r = -.05$ at age nineteen) are substantially lower than that between early viewing of violence and later aggression. Furthermore, partial correlation techniques similar to those used in the previously described study, whereby the correlations between television violence and aggression were computed while the alternative possible causal variables were controlled, such as IQ, social class, parental punishment and parental aggression, did not yield substantially reduced correlations. This indicates that none of these additional variables can account for the observed relationship.

84

Partial correlation provides a means of examining plausible alternative explanations to the hypothesis that television violence causes aggression. One possibility is that aggression at age nine leads both to heavy viewing of violent television at age nine and to aggression at age nineteen. A fact that supports this possible explanation is that there is a substantial correlation between aggression at age nine and aggression at age nineteen ($r = +.38$). Dr Eron and his co-workers agree that early aggression probably does contribute to later aggression. However, their main interest is in whether or not the relationship between early television preferences for television and later aggression can be explained as an artifact of early aggression. To examine this possibility they computed the partial correlation between television violence at nine and aggression at nineteen while controlling for aggression at nine. This gives us an indication of what the relationship between early viewing and later aggression would be if early aggression were not involved. If our alternative explanation is correct, that is, that early aggression causes both early viewing habits and later aggression, the partial correlation would be zero. In fact it is $+.25$, which is only .06 below the original correlation between early preference for violence and later aggression. Thus the alternative hypothesis appears to be implausible as a complete explanation, although early aggression may make a contribution to subsequent aggressiveness in young people, as one might expect.

Dr Eron's research team conclude that their analysis demonstrates a probable causative influence of watching violent television programmes in the early formative years of childhood on later aggression. They are careful not to claim that television violence is the only cause of aggressive behaviour, and point out that many other factors are related to aggression. However, their findings do indicate an influence of television violence on aggression, irrespective of any effects of other variables, and show that television violence accounts for a larger proportion of the variance than any single alternative factor considered in the investigation, which included measures of IQ, social class, religion, ethnic background and parental disharmony.

Survey techniques cannot provide entirely watertight evidence on the matter, but taken as a whole the survey evidence is undoubtedly consistent with the assertion that television violence does influence children. This assertion provides the simplest and most likely explanation of the data that have been collected. The studies I have described are only a sample of the survey research that has been undertaken, but no large-scale recent studies provide evidence which would contradict the present conclusion. Some investigators would demur with this judgement, and we shall bring

85

up some objections and problems later, after considering alternative kinds of evidence on the effects of television violence. One particular qualification should be mentioned. This is the fact that the magnitudes of the observed relationships between measures of viewing and measures of aggression are generally too low to permit us to make useful predictions about the effects of television violence upon individuals. Generally speaking, the observed correlations are not much above +.3, and even if they were due entirely to a direct causal connection between television violence and behaviour, this knowledge would make our estimates of a particular child's aggressive behaviour only around ten per cent more accurate, on average, than simple guessing.

Experimental findings

In undertaking experiments, which generally form the preferred method of psychologists interested in assessing the effects of television violence, some of the limitations of survey techniques are avoided. Experiments have been carried out in large numbers, and their findings show with no shadow of a doubt that children's behaviour can be influenced by the actions of people they see on television and cinema screens. However, the majority of such studies are too artificial, insofar that their conditions are unlike those in which children's day-to-day watching of television at home, for it to be realistic to use the findings as the sole basis for confident statements about the actual effects of everyday television viewing.

Experimental research into socialization has stressed the importance of learning for the acquisition of social habits. The child watches someone in a certain way and later imitates his behaviour. The term 'Model' is normally used to denote the individual whose actions are observed and, perhaps, subsequently imitated. Numerous experiments on social learning have been conducted in the United States by Albert Bandura and by his students. Bandura, who has been President of the American Psychological Association, and who is unarguably among the most distinguished of those social scientists whose research has a direct bearing upon the effects of television violence, had the distinction of being blacklisted in 1969 by representatives of the US television networks when it was proposed that he should sit on the United States Surgeon General's Committee formed to inquire into the influence of television crime and violence.

Typical of the earlier experiments undertaken in Bandura's laboratory is one involving ninety-six children in a nursery school, aged between
86

three and five years. (10) Some of the children were assigned at random to an experimental condition in which they were first taken into a room and allowed to settle down with some toys. Subsequently, an adult who was also in the room began playing with the toys. These included a large inflated doll, five feet high, weighted at the bottom, which the adult began hitting with a mallet. The adult model's aggressive actions towards the doll took the form of behaviours that were deliberately distinctive and new to the children, and each act was repeated on a number of occasions during the session, while the child watched what was going on.

Children who had been allocated to the second experimental condition were placed in the same room, given identical toys, and they then watched a film show. In the film the same adult model seen by the children in the first group was shown with the identical inflated doll and the model went through an identical sequence of novel and aggressive actions. Children in a third condition also watched a film. This was designed to be like a cartoon, and involved fantasy settings and an adult in cat's costume who acted aggressively towards the doll which featured in the other experimental conditions. A further group of children served as a control condition, for purposes of comparison, and they did not witness aggressive behaviour.

Afterwards, each child was taken to another room, containing a number of very attractive toys, and was told he could play with them. However, as soon as play began the child was informed by the experimenter that she had decided to reserve the toys for some other children, and the child was taken to a different room in which there were a number of ordinary toys, together with a doll like the one which most of the children had seen earlier, and a mallet. The child was observed for twenty minutes, to see how he would react to this frustrating turn of events. Judges observed his behaviour through a one-way mirror. This enabled them to watch him from the next room, although he could not see them.

The aim of the investigation was to discover whether or not prior exposure to adult aggression would influence the children's reaction to being frustrated. In fact it did have a marked effect. When the total number of aggressive responses was calculated, the children in the control group received an average aggression score of 54, compared with 82 for the children who watched the live model behaving aggressively, 92 for those children who watched the real person in the film, and 99 for those children who saw the cartoon film. Many of the particular aggressive actions clearly copied those of the models, the amount of imitation being greater among those who had watched real adults, either live or on film than among those children who saw the cartoon film. In short, it is clear that in appropriate circumstances children certainly can and do imitate the aggressive acts they see being performed by adults.

A second example of the experimental research carried out by Bandura and his collaborators into the acquisition of aggressive social habits through observing and imitating models, involved children of similar ages, averaging just over four years. (11) Some of the children watched a film, shown on television, involving two men. In the film one of the men, Johnny, is playing with some attractive toys, and the other man, Rocky, asks if he also can play. Johnny refuses, whereupon Rocky begins to be physically and verbally aggressive towards Johnny and his toys. As in the previous study, the particular acts of aggression were chosen to be highly distinctive and novel to the children, making it possible for observers to rate directly imitative aggressive responses and to distinguish them from aggressive actions already within a child's repertoire. As a result of being aggressive, Rocky is victorious, and as he is announced as the victor he can be seen playing happily with the toys, and simultaneously enjoying his favourite food and drink. Meanwhile, Johnny sits alone in a corner, dejected.

Other children saw a different film. This one involved the same characters, Rocky and Johnny, and included identical aggressive acts. This time, however, Rocky's aggressive behaviour is less successful. He is beaten by Johnny, who emerges victorious, and this version ends with Rocky sitting dejected in a corner of the room without any toys.

Following each of the experimental conditions, every child was observed for twenty minutes as he played in a different room. This contained a number of toys, some of which were identical to ones seen in the film, and some of which were not. During this session the average score for aggressive behaviour among children who had seen the aggressive model rewarded was 75, compared with 54 among the children who had seen the other film, and 62 among children in a control group who saw neither film. Thus it does appear to be the case that seeing a model rewarded for being aggressive results in a greater amount of imitative aggression than seeing an adult model whose aggressive actions are not rewarded. Later on, the children who participated in this experiment were asked which of the two characters they preferred. Children who had seen Rocky as the victor chose him on sixty per cent of occasions, while only five per cent chose Johnny. However, those children who had watched the film in which Rocky was unsuccessful chose the two characters equally often. Those children who preferred Rocky were not unaware of the anti-social nature of his behaviour. Their statements indicate that some were even attracted by his villainy, especially when he ended up the winner. As one four-year-old said, 'Rocky is harsh. I be harsh like he was'.

The above findings show that whether a model is rewarded or not influences the likelihood of his actions being imitated by a young child. It is conceivable that even when non-rewarded acts are not imitated they are nonetheless learned, and may be performed by the child on subsequent occasions. An experiment was designed to examine this possibility. (12) Once more, the children were around four years of age. Each saw one of three films on television. In one film the adult model was rewarded for acting aggressively towards a large doll in the form of a clown. This model, in the film, was told he was a 'Strong champion' and given large quantities of sweets and fizzy drinks. In the second film the model's aggressive actions, which paralleled those seen in the first film, were less successful. He was called a bully by the other adult, sat upon and struck, and he ended by running off while he was threatened with a spanking if he was caught acting in the same way again. The third film showed only the first section of the sequence. The model acted aggressively, but the film terminated without any overt consequences for the adult's behaviour.

Subsequently, each child was observed, and, as we might expect the children who saw the model rewarded and those who watched the film in which there were no consequences of the aggressive actions displayed more imitative aggression than the children who watched the film in which the model was punished. Girls imitated the aggressive actions less than did the boys. Next, however, the experimenter asked all the children to show her what the model had done on the television film, and at this stage she provided a range of attractive items as rewards for the children. The findings indicate that the amount of spontaneous imitation demonstrated previously by no means provided a complete picture of the amount of imitation of which they were capable. At this later stage children in each of the three groups were shown to be capable of a greater number of imitative actions than they had demonstrated earlier. Not only did the previous difference between the groups in number of aggressive imitations disappear, but so did the difference between boys and girls. Girls were able to copy virtually as many aggressive acts as the boys.

In sum, these findings suggest that whilst the consequences of aggression that children have witnessed may have some influence, affecting the amount and extent of spontaneous imitation in the period immediately following observation, the consequences to the model do not affect the likelihood of aggressive acts entering the children's repertoires, and becoming available for subsequent use when required.

As I have said previously, there are limitations in the extent to which we can use the findings of experiments much as the one just described as evidence of the effects of violence seen on television in children's daily lives. One particular limitation of the experiments we have so far described is that the measures of child aggression were obtained in the context of play behaviours which did not involve a real person being hurt. It may be that a child's aggressive actions towards toys or dolls give a poor indication of the extent to which the same child would be aggressive or violent towards real people. Experiments to be described in the pages immediately following attempted to surmount this problem by arranging experimental situations in which the child was led to believe that his aggressive actions really were hurting or harming another individual. In devising such situations it has been found possible to arrive at experimental arrangements which although artificial are not seen as being so by the child. In other words the child thinks that the circumstances are realistic, and not part of an experiment. This gives an important element of reality to the experiment, having implications for the applicability of the findings however far from natural life the devious experimenter has really departed in order to conduct his study.

Some aspects of everyday television viewing cannot be satisfactorily duplicated in laboratory experiments, however ingenious the social scientist. One problem lies in the fact that daily viewing of television takes place at home, in an environment that is completely familiar and in which the child can move freely, using television as and when fancy directs him. Another difficulty is that the effects of long-term and regular viewing are likely to be cumulative, and different from the immediate outcome of one short presentation. Experiments to measure immediate and short-term effects of a particular film or programme can easily be designed, but neither regular or long term viewing, nor measurement of its effects, can be entirely satisfactorily incorporated in laboratory experiments. However, the experimental field studies to be described later constitute attempts to duplicate these aspects of everyday television viewing.

Among the recent experimental studies measuring what the child subjects believed to be real interpersonal aggression is an investigation carried out in Ohio by R M Liebert and R A Baron. (13) The participants were children between five and nine years of age. When a child arrived the experimenter asked to be excused for a few minutes in order to attend to some urgent business and suggested that the child should watch television while waiting for him to return. During this period the

90

child was continuously observed through a concealed video camera. Each child first saw two innocuous commercials, selected for their humour and attention-gaining qualities. Next some of the children watched an excerpt lasting about three minutes from a violent television series, *The Untouchables*. The short extract contained a chase, two fist-fighting scenes, two shootings and a knifing. The other children watched an active but non-violent sequence depicting events. Afterwards each participant saw another commercial, and as it ended the experimenter re-entered the room and told the child that she was ready to begin. The whole television-viewing session had been carefully arranged so as to give the child the impression that it was merely for filling time while he waited for the experimenter to be ready for him.

Each child was then taken to another room, and his attention was drawn to a gray metal box upon which were a white light and two buttons, one green and one red. Beneath the red button was printed the word 'Hurt', and the word 'Help' was below the green button. Wires ran from the box to the adjoining wall. Each child was told that a game was under way in the next room. In the game the player would turn a handle, and doing this would illuminate the white light on the metal box. The child was told that when the white light came on he could do one of two things. Either he could push the green button, in which case the handle in the next room would be easier to turn, thus helping a child player there to win his game. Alternatively, the red button could be pushed, and the outcome of this would be to make the handle next door feel hot, hurting the player and forcing him to let go of it. The instructions were explained very carefully, the experimenter repeating herself if necessary, to ensure that the child really understood. It was explained that the child could go on pushing the same button on each trial, or change from one to the other, as he preferred. The child was also told that the longer he pushed the green button the more he helped the child player next door, and the longer he pushed the red button, the more the other child would be hurt.

After being assured that the child subject understood the task the experimenter left the room. During the subsequent few minutes the lights were illuminated sufficiently often to produce twenty trials, separated from each other by intervals of fifteen seconds. The responses made by each subject were registered automatically. The primary measure of aggression was based upon the total duration of each child's 'Hurt' responses during the twenty trials. No significant differences emerged between boys and girls, or between the younger (aged five and six years) and older (aged eight and nine) children participating in the experiment. However, there was a large difference between subjects in the two experimental conditions. Children who had seen the aggressive television programme subsequently engaged in considerably more interpersonal aggression than those who watched the neutral programme. On average, the duration of aggressive responses was about fifty per cent more among children who saw the violent contents than among the other children. They did not, on the whole, make a larger number of 'Hurt' responses, but their 'Hurts' were of considerably longer duration.

Before accepting the conclusion that these findings provide a clear demonstration of increased aggression, Liebert and Baron looked into some plausible alternative explanations. One possibility is that the higher aggression scores obtained by those children who watched the violent programmes were due to them simply having become more aroused than the children in the other group. But if this were the case one would expect the group of subjects who saw the aggressive programme to yield larger 'Help' scores than the others, in addition to their great 'Hurt' measures. As it happens the findings show no difference between groups in 'Help' scores, indicating that this alternative explanation is incorrect.

Drs Liebert and Baron are careful to avoid making any unjustified conclusions from their findings. As they point out, the overall results of the experiment provide 'relatively consistent evidence for the view that certain aspects of a child's willingness to aggress may be at least temporarily increased by merely witnessing aggressive television programmes'. (13) They note that the main effect of exposure to aggression in the present experiment was to increase the magnitude of the hurting response, by reducing children's restraints against inflicting violence on another child.

There exists a number of further research findings which support the view that exposure to violent content can lead a child to commit violent acts towards others. In a number of earlier experiments various groups of subjects watched a knife-fight sequence from the film *Rebel Without a Cause*. Later they were placed in a situation in which they were led to believe they were required to administer electric shocks to other individuals whenever they made errors on a test of learning. After seeing the film, the adolescent boys who participated as subjects, among others, gave stronger shocks than participants who watched an alternative film that showed constructive activities. In a similar experiment it was discovered that boys who had a past history of delinquent behaviour acted more aggressively than the others. Another investigation showed that while both male university students and male inmates in a prison for violent criminals gave stronger shocks after watching violent contents than comparable

92

individuals in a control group, the prisoners were more aggressive than the students. Predictable though this latter finding might seem, it serves a purpose in that it supports the notion that the kinds of aggression exhibited in the necessarily unnatural situations used in experiments of this kind are not unrelated to violence in real life. Their results therefore have a definite bearing upon violence and aggression.

The experiments on aggression that have been described up to this point have each examined the effects of events upon the behaviour of the subject. Earlier in the chapter it was pointed out that there may be ill effects of television violence in addition to that of increasing the viewer's own aggressive behaviour. One possibility is that individuals become more tolerant of violence in others. A second is that a person's perception of violent and aggressive acts may become blurred. The findings of two recent studies have a bearing upon these suggestions.

In a very ingenious investigation reported by an American team of researchers, Ronald Drabman and Margaret Thomas, in 1974 (14), the experimenter met each of the nine- and ten-year-old participants individually in their school classroom. He told each child that he was ahead of schedule, and to fill time proposed showing him his 'new trailer', a large mobile caravan. This was placed in the school playground, and the experimenter explained to the child that it was sometimes used by a friend who was working with younger kindergarten-age children from another school. On opening the door, the trailer was found to contain a room in which there was a collection of young children's toys, such as blocks, crayons and toy milk bottles. At one end there was a large television camera. It was explained that this was permanently switched on, and recorded everything that happened in the room.

Next, the experimenter and the child went back to a room in the main school building, to play the games that provided the ostensible purpose for the experimental session. At one stage some of the children saw an eight-minute violent Western, which contained several gun-battles, shootings and fights. Immediately afterwards, the experimenter casually looked at his watch and then told the child that he had to make an important phone call. He also explained to the child that there was a slight problem, because he had previously promised the friend who worked with kindergarten children in the trailer that he would look after some children there while the friend had to be away. The experimenter then pointed to a television set in the room and showed that this was monitoring the trailer, which was now empty. He showed relief that the younger children had not yet arrived there, and after telling the child that it was possible they might arrive before

93

he returned from making the telephone call, he asked the child if he would be willing to watch the children on television, if they did return. The child participants invariably agreed to do so, and the experimenter then went on to repeat that the child should just watch the screen, and if the younger children did arrive, keep an eye on them. He continued, 'I imagine they'll be OK, but sometimes little kids can get into trouble, and that's why an older person should be watching them. If anything *does* happen, come and get me. I'll be in the principal's office.'

At this point in the experiment each child saw an identical videotaped sequence on television. Having originally shown each child the television camera while they were looking at the play area in the trailer, the experimenter could be fairly confident that the child would believe the events he saw to be genuinely live. The videotape shows the inside of the trailer. At first it is seen to be unoccupied. Then a male adult and two young children enter. The adult tells the children that he has to leave, and that they can play while he is gone. The children then play quietly on their own for about a minute, and then each makes a building with the blocks. One of them, the girl, criticises the structures the boy has made. This leads to a sequence of insults on each side and afterwards the boy maliciously knocks over one of the girl's buildings. They continue arguing, and destroy the remaining buildings. Then they start pushing and threatening each other. The girl starts to cry, at the same time chasing the boy, while he taunts her, shouting 'you can't catch me'. She hits him several times, and they struggle close to the camera. Then it appears to the viewer that the camera is knocked to the floor, the video signal goes dead, while the sound continues briefly, conveying shouted accusations of blame. Finally, after a shout of 'Watch out' by the boy, there is a loud crash, followed by silence.

While the child was watching all this, the experimenter waited in the hallway outside the room, stopwatch in hand, and he recorded the elapsed time between the onset of the tape and the moment at which the subject left the room to call attention to what he believed was going on in the trailer. In computing the results, the researcher subtracted from these time values the period of time that had elapsed in the videotape prior to the initial aggressive acts, that is, knocking the first blocks down. The resulting time scores thus provide a measure of the length of time during which the subject watched the aggressive incident before reporting it.

The children who participated as subjects were then carefully debriefed. They were assured that the man in charge of the kindergarten
94

children had now returned and that no real harm had been done. Each child then took part in an 'experiment' consisting of a maze-solving task, and was praised and rewarded with confectionery.

The experimental findings show that watching the violent film did strikingly increase participants' toleration of aggressive behaviour in the kindergarten children. The length of time that went by before the fighting was reported averaged 112 seconds for the children who watched the violent film, compared with 69 seconds for the others. Boys and girls did not appreciably differ. A further analysis took the form of separating the scores in order to divide subjects who had sought help as a response to the children's arguing and destruction of property, before the more extreme forms of aggression, such as fighting, began, from those who had not gone for help until after matters had become really violent. Among the children who had not seen the violent film, eleven of the subjects went to get help in the first phase, and eight waited until the more extreme forms of aggression occurred. However, among the participants who did see the violent film, only three sought help before the high levels of physical violence were observed, and fifteen delayed reporting the incident until afterwards.

In short, these findings indicate that children's responsiveness to what they believe to be real physical aggression in others can be influenced by observing violence on television. Drs Drabman and Thomas, the investigators, suggest that if children use what they see on television as a guide to how life really is—and, as we have seen, they certainly do—watching aggressive and violent acts may indeed make children more likely to regard conflict and fighting as normal and acceptable human behaviours.

To discover whether television can affect children's degree of sensitivity to violent acts, and an experiment was carried out in which violent and non-violent films were shown to American twelve-year-olds. (6) After seeing the films each child looked at pictures shown very briefly, two at a time by a projector normally used for presenting stereoscopic effects. The pictures in each pair appeared simultaneously, but so briefly that only one of the two could be seen. The two images were very similar in form and texture, except that one showed a violent act and the other did not. For instance, in one slide a man struck another on the head with a gun, and in the corresponding picture another man in the same location and a similar position helped another person make a hole in the ground, using the butt of a gun.

After viewing each pair of slides, the child was asked to describe in writing what he had seen. It was found that the children who had just

95

seen the violent film less frequently reported violent incidents shown on the slides than the other subjects, indicating that, temporarily at least, they had become less sensitive to the visual depiction of violent acts. Of course, further research would be necessary to determine whether seeing violence on television also has a long-term effect of blunting children's sensitivity in addition to the immediate influence demonstrated in this study. However, the findings of the present investigation do provide grounds for suggesting that repeated viewing is likely to have a long-term influence.

Taken as a whole, the evidence from laboratory experiments proves that children can be influenced by what they see on television, at least over short periods of time. As Albert Bandura has remarked, the laboratory findings 'do not present a pretty picture, unless our society is interested in increasing the aggressive tendencies of a growing generation.'(15)

Findings of field experiments

A major advantage of field studies is that it is normally possible to consider long-term influences, and to look into the outcomes of continuous or regular contact with the television medium over a period of weeks or months, rather than minutes, as in the typical laboratory experiment. In laboratory studies time restrictions are usually in force; one can rarely expect subjects to inconvenience themselves for more than an hour or two, and facilities for looking after their needs over longer periods are very expensive and usually unavailable.

One large-scale field study is particularly interesting since it was conducted by researchers who confidently believed that long term exposure to violent television would decrease rather than increase aggression in children, contrary to the expectations of most scientists engaged in research in this field. It did yield some results which appear to support the unorthodox belief. The claim was that seeing televised violence can have an effect of 'catharsis'. Applied to aggression, the notion of catharsis implies that the witnessing of aggressive acts, possibly in fantasy form, can reduce a person's 'aggressive drive'. Increased drive is supposed to create tension and unpleasant feelings, but these can be reduced either by aggressive actions or through vicarious means, of which witnessing violence is one.

This kind of account, and the implicit 'hydraulic' model of aggression as a quantity that somehow swells up to produce extreme pressures which need to be released either through direct action or through an alternative outlet of 'safety valve', is by no means new. Aristotle, for instance,

96

wrote about the purgative effects of drama, whereby the audience is permitted to release various intense feelings and emotions. Freud, who pointed out that one of the costs of living in an organized society is the inhibition of free expression of aggressive impulses, claimed that there exists an aggressive instinct which constantly presses for discharge through aggressive behaviour.

Seymour Fesbach and Robert Singer (16) claim that having aggressive fantasies, and seeing aggression in others, can lower the probability of a person acting violently. They note that individuals are often deprived of things they want, or do not get them soon enough. Furthermore they may be insulted, physically attacked, or demeaned in some other way, and under circumstances of this kind they may act aggressively. However, a variety of constraints prevent people from acting violently every time they feel aggressive. Fear of punishment, shame, guilt, retaliation, social disapproval all tend to counterbalance aggressive impulses. The resulting dilemma can be reduced in any of a number of ways, for example through dreams, daydreams and other fantasy activities. For instance a man may daydream about how he is going to tell off his boss, or attack his mother-in-law.

Television fantasy aggression is regarded by these authors as providing materials that facilitate cognitive control of behaviour. We might think of the ability to fantasize as being an adaptive mechanism for coping with frustrations of various kinds. If this is so, it is likely that some people, particularly those with a 'low fantasy ability' will be likely to benefit from the fantasy provided by external sources such as television. In particular, it is claimed that children of low intelligence and limited imagination, who are unable to maufacture their own fantasy lives from everyday experience, will benefit from fantasy materials provided by the medium of television. Furthermore, so the argument goes, the long-term effect for these children's watching television violence will be to decrease rather than increase their levels of aggressive behaviour.

This line of reasoning is not without logical inconsistencies, and over the years has received very little support in attempts to verify it by empirical research. However, Fesbach and Singer, undeterred, undertook a lengthy and ambitious field study, involving measurement of the effects of violent and non-violent television content on a large sample of boys living in a variety of residential institutions in the United States. Some of the boys were from middle class families, living in private boarding schools, and others came from poorer backgrounds. Some were emotionally disturbed, and lived in homes for individuals who had difficulties in coping with life or who lacked adequate care in their own families.

Over a period of six weeks each boy's television viewing was restricted to programmes from a list of items that were either all violent or all non-violent. Half of the boys had to choose from a list of 75 programmes all of which contained violence and physical aggression. The list included Westerns, spy series and other 'action' features. The others chose from a list of non-violent programmes, which included variety, humour and sport. Assessments of the boys' own aggressive behaviour were contributed by house-parents and by teachers.

Difference in the aggression scores between the two experimental groups tended to be small, but in three of the seven institutions the boys who watched the violent television programmes over the six weeks period acted, on the whole, less aggressively towards both their peers and towards the authorities than the other boys. Thus for these boys, the catharsis hypothesis receives some support from the experimental findings.

There are some puzzling features of this experiment, however, which incline one to question the catharsis explanation of the results. Other studies have consistently failed to find any reduction in aggressiveness following the viewing of violent programmes, and in the present investigation it is noticeable that the beneficial effects of violence occurred only in the institutions for disturbed or deprived boys, and not in the middle class schools. It is a well known fact that boys like violent television programmes, preferring them, on the whole, to non-violent ones, and findings of the attitude surveys we reviewed in chapter two suggest that boys in the groups who became more aggressive following the non-violent programme diet would have been those with the strongest initial preference for violent programmes and hence the most strongly frustrated by not being allowed to watch them. The authors are somewhat equivocal about this. They admit to a concern that the boys might have resented being assigned to the non-aggressive diet, but appear to discount the possibility that such frustration might have led to increased aggressiveness, thus influencing the experimental findings. However, an indication that very real frustration, probably giving rise to aggression, was at least temporarily induced by preventing boys from seeing the violent series they liked is provided by the admission in the report that some of the boys in the non-violent programme group objected so strongly to being prevented from seeing *Batman* that it was added to the list of programmes they were allowed to watch. Including *Batman* in the list severely compromised the experimental design, the possible effect being like that of allowing

98

participants in a test of the effectiveness of a sugar-free diet to eat a bar of chocolate every day, and one can be sure that the experimenters would not have given in to such a demand unless they felt they absolutely had to. One can guess that if the boys' protests against the violence-free television diet were sufficiently strong to force the experimenters to modify the experiment in this crucial and undesirable manner, the reactions to the prohibition must have been very forceful indeed. Furthermore, the investigators' act of yielding to the protests may well have encouraged the participants to be assertively aggressive in other ways, and may have increased the numbers of complaints and rule breaking incidents, each of which were counted in calculating a boy's aggression scores.

The fact that this field experiment contains obvious flaws does not necessarily render it valueless. Few experimental studies are entirely flawless, and experimental field studies, which necessitate the close co-operation of a number of individuals, researchers, teachers and other supervisory and domestic staff, and the reconciling of their differing and not always compatible responsibilities, are notorious for producing problems that threaten to undermine the controls built into planned research. However, the irregularities in this particular study are too striking to be easily dismissed. Equally important is the fact that a recent replication of the experiment produced a reversed pattern of findings. Significantly more physical aggressiveness was observed among boys who saw the violent programmes. The only evidence from the later study that might possible be claimed to support the catharsis hypothesis was the finding that individuals who watched only the non-violent programmes were more verbally aggressive than the others. However, it appears that most of the increased verbal aggression took the form of complaints about the 'lousy' programmes to which the boys were restricted!

One final experiment is of interest, both because it provides an unusually carefully designed study of the effects of television violence upon young children, three to five years of age, and also because it combines its observations of the effects of violence with measures of the influence of programme contents designed to produce definite 'prosocial' effects that contribute to qualities such as altruism, cooperation and self-control. The latter aspect of the experiment will be discussed at length in the next chapter. At this point we shall briefly survey those findings which concern the outcome of the violent programmes shown, *Batman* and *Superman*.

Ninety-two children attending a nursery school were involved in the experiment, and it was conducted by Lynette Friedrich and Aletha Stein during a nine-week Summer Term. (17) During the first two weeks

99

baseline scores were established for each child's habitual behaviour. Then the children were divided into three groups, who watched different kinds of television shows over the next four weeks. The three types of programmes were aggressive, neutral or prosocial. The effects of viewing were assessed during the final week of the term. It was found that those children, of both sexes, who were initially more aggressive than average showed greater interpersonal aggression after being exposed to the aggressive programme contents than similar children exposed to neutral or prosocial contents. Children who were initially less aggressive were not differentially influenced by the three conditions, so far as their aggression scores were concerned. The observers who measured aggressive behaviours did not know to which condition the child they were observing had been assigned. Grounds for believing that these findings apply directly to real life are provided by the fact that measurement of children's aggression was undertaken at a time and in a place removed from the viewing experience and by the fact that natural, everyday aggression was measured, rather than participants' responses to particular situations. Furthermore, it should be noted that a significant effect endured for some weeks at least, following exposure to an amount of television content that was very small (a total of twelve programmes over the four-week period) in relation to the amount the children regularly viewed at home. These findings supply evidence that is very hard to refute for the assertion that violent television contents do appreciably influence some children's behaviour. The observation that the children who were previously aggressive were the ones who were influenced by television violence is consistent with other evidence that these children are the ones who are most at risk in this respect.

Having surveyed a representative selection of recent investigations based upon surveys, laboratory experiments and field experiments, we should be able to decide whether or not the available facts warrant a firm conclusion about the effects of television violence on children. Does it cause children to be more aggressive?

No one study can provide cast-iron evidence that television violence does affect children over an extended period of time, although some investigations, such as the one by Friedrich and Stein, would make a very convincing case, even if alternative forms of evidence did not exist. But taking the findings of all applicable research as a whole, the consensus of results provides what by any realistic scientific criterion amounts to an extremely strong body of support for the statement that television violence not only can but does affect some children, making them more

100

aggressive than they would be otherwise. My considered judgement is that the case is conclusively proved. Survey findings strongly point to such a conclusion, as also do the results of laboratory experiments and those of the more true-to-life field experimental studies. The one large-scale study which has produced some results that appear to contradict these generalizations has serious deficiencies, and its discrepant findings are not supported by the data obtained from a replication of it.

Dissenting views

The written statements of the vast majority of independent scientists who have undertaken empirical research into the effects of television violence indicate agreement with this conclusion. Indeed, it is extremely hard to think of plausible alternative interpretations of the available evidence. However, some views have been expressed which demur with this judgement, and they are worthy of attention.

A British researcher, Dennis Howitt, and an American, Richard Dembo, advance what they term a 'Subcultural account' of media effects. (18) They argue that concern over the role of the mass media as producers of violence outweighs any contribution the media have in influencing behaviour, and that social scientists who want to find the major causes of violence and aggression should look elsewhere. Howitt and Dembo consider that many of the available research findings can be explained by reference to 'the behaviour patterns of so-called delinquent sub-cultures'. They note that cinema, comic books and pop music, which are associated with aggression and delinquency all represent valued activities among young people orientated to street culture. They also claim that the beliefs and activities of these adolescents, whose life chances force them to live in static social circumstances, contrast with the achievement orientation and behaviour of other young people striving for upward mobility. The socially static youngsters, mainly working class, develop alternative means of achieving self-esteem, and many of these are based upon the values and pursuits of the street culture. One proves one's 'hardness', for example, by success at roles demanding physical and sexual prowess, and by success at certain sports, for example, soccer and boxing.

As evidence for their point of view, these authors cite the findings of a small-scale study carried out to investigate social behaviour and patterns of media use among boys aged between twelve and fifteen in the North-East of England. Peer ratings of aggressive behaviour did not differentiate the youths in terms of exposure to the eight forms of mass media that were considered. On the other hand, a measure of street culture

101

orientation did correlate significantly with cinema attendance and use of pop music.

The concept of a street culture has undoubted utility for attempts to understand the causes of violence in the young, and consideration of it serves to remind us to be wary of assuming that any factor contributing to aggression can operate entirely in isolation from other societal influences. However, what is known about street culture cannot in any important respect be regarded as contradicting the evidence which has led us to conclude that television violence leads to increased aggression. It may well be that differences between individuals in degree of aggressiveness are also related to street culture variables. But as we have seen, the correlation between viewing and violence is not seriously decreased when partial correlation techniques are used to remove the possible contributions of a number of factors also related to social class and family background— factors which are closely involved in measures of street culture. Acceptance of the view that a youth's degree of adherence to the values of a street culture may influence his aggression by no means contradicts the conclusion that watching violence on television leads to increases in aggressive behaviour and influences attitudes towards the place of violence in human life.

The reminder that aggression is multiply determined brings to mind a consideration that might incline us to qualify the view that the research findings provide entirely conclusive evidence of television's causative influences on aggression in British children. The vast majority of the research undertaken into the effects of television violence has been done in the United States, which is a more violent society than Britain. Furthermore, there are differences in television content. American channels broadcast larger quantities of violence, and provide less high-quality non-violent programming. In extrapolating American-based research findings to Britain we make a cross-cultural leap which, so far as violence is concerned, may be substantial. My own considred guess is that if the American investigations were replicated in Britain, the findings would be practically the same, but lacking appropriate evidence, it is not possible to be certain about this. Further British investigations are required, especially ones taking the form of experimental research.

Since it is tolerably certain that present levels of television violence do adversely affect some children, we ought to do all we can to ensure that some things are changed. There is no justification for the amounts of violence that are now permitted. But whenever it has been suggested that television violence should be substantially reduced, counter-
102

arguments have been raised. One is the bland assertion that efforts have been made and are being made to control the permitted quantities of television violence. To support this claim, reference has been made to codes on violence introduced by the television companies, and to recent extensions of such codes. In fact, although it may be possible to produce statistics which point to deductions from levels of violent content permitted some years ago, it is only necessary to watch television over a period of a few days, (*any* few days will do) to discover that, even in Britain, levels of gratuitous violence and viciousness remain strikingly high, and the most recent survey findings definitely confirm this impression. Present circumstances in Britain may not be so bad as they could be, or so bad as they have been, or as bad as in the United States. Nevertheless it is undoubtedly true that harmful levels of violence are still permitted, and while the means for changing this situation are readily available, there is no excuse for not removing this source of harm to our children.

Another argument used to oppose reducing violence levels is that we ought to do nothing until we are one hundred per cent certain of its harmful consequences. This is a little like suggesting that Britain should not have started defending itself against Germany until it was absolutely certain that Hitler would invade. The principle that commodities should be banned or restricted when there exists a high probability of their being harmful, although no certain proof, is a widely accepted one. Cigarette advertising is restricted, various drugs are banned, as are numerous food additives, on the basis of evidence that harmful effects are highly probable.

Yet another argument against limiting violence is that such restrictions will drive audiences away. As we have remarked, many programmes containing high levels of violence are very popular, among both children and adults. If any one US network or British television company acted alone, the effect might well be to reduce its audience, and any broadcasting company has reasons, not only commercial ones, for wanting to retain its viewers. As David Attenborough has said, on behalf of the BBC, 'It's no good going out on the blasted heath and speaking in the most marvellous aphorisms if nobody is listening'. If substantial changes are to be introduced in the quantity of violence permitted on television they have to be made at a national level. In the United States the lobbying power of commercial interests makes this difficult, but in Britain, where considerable national control can relatively easily be exerted over the independent television companies as well as over the BBC, there is no real justification for inaction.

103

A final ploy used in arguments against the limitation of violence is to bring up the bogey of censorship, suggesting that restrictions constitute assaults upon the freedom of individuals. We certainly must be aware of the possible limits to our freedom which any form of control entails, but this is no reason for failing to protect our children from known sources of harm. To protect ourselves and our society we have to restrict freedom of action in all kinds of ways. We drive on only one side of the road, we don't throw sewage onto the streets and we permit all kinds of laws and regulations that place limits on people's activities. Genuine concern about the dangers of censorship is basically a matter of concern about interference to freedom of legitimate self-expression. Restricting violence is a very different matter.

Sex and the small screen

The major intention of writing this book has been to survey the available knowledge concerning how children are affected by what they see and hear on television. Television presents some materials containing a sexual element, ranging from 'blue' jokes and double entendres to the occasional full-frontal nude episode, and broadcasting companies are sometimes accused of presenting aspects of sex in a manner that is harmful to children. Therefore it seemed appropriate to include a summary of the known evidence about the effects of televised sex on children.

As it happened, my search for hard facts on this matter drew a virtual blank. There may be some truth in the assertion that children are harmed by television's depictions of sexual aspects of life, or there may be no truth in it at all. One just cannot tell, since there is a lack of objective information. The necessary scientific investigations that would be required in order to provide reliable and valid evidence have not yet been undertaken.

This situation may be remedied in the future, although research into the effects of portraying sex presents some problems in addition to those encountered in investigations of, say, the effects of television violence. In the case of violence one can identify a number of possible outcomes for which there exists practically unanimous agreement about their undesirability. For instance, few people in Britain would disagree with the assertion that it is wrong for a child to act violently towards others, except in self-defence. However, in the case of sex on television, it would not be so easy to obtain agreement about what constitutes undesirable outcomes, unless one considers only the most extreme manifestations, such as an increase in the incidence of rape.

104

At least for the present, the informed answer to questions asking about the possible influence on children of those aspects of sex that are portrayed in television programmes is that we simply do not know.

REFERENCES

1 Glucksman, A: *Violence on the screen,* translated by Susan Bennet. London: British Film Institute, 1971.

2 Shulman, M: *The ravenous eye.* London: Cassell, 1973.

3 Siegal, A: The effects of media violence on social learning. Pp 613–636 in Schramm, W, and Roberts, D F (eds): *The process and effects of mass communication.* Revised edition. Urbana, Illinois: University of Chicago Press, 1971.

4 Himmelweit, H T, Oppenheim, A N, and Vince, P: *Television and the child.* London: Oxford University Press 1958.

5 Schramm, W, Lyle, J, and Parker, E: *Television in the lives of our children.* Stanford, California: Stanford University Press, 1961.

6 Atkin, C K, Murray, J P, and Nayman, O B: The Surgeon General's research program on television and social behavior: a review of empirical findings. *Journal of broadcasting,* 16, Winter 1971–72, pp 21–35.

7 Greenberg, B S: British children and television violence. *Public opinion quarterly,* 1974.

8 Lefkowitz, M M, Walder, L O, Eron, L D and Huesman, L R: Preference for televised contact sports as related to sex differences in aggression. *Developmental psychology,* 9, 1973, pp 417–420.

9 Eron, L D, Huesmann, L R, Lefkowitz, M M, and Walder, L O: Does television violence cause aggression? *American psychologist,* 27, 1972, pp 253–263.

10 Bandura, A, Ross, D, and Ross, S A: Imitation of film-mediated aggressive models. *Journal of abnormal and social psychology,* 66, 1963, pp 3–11.

11 Bandura, A, Ross, D, and Ross, S A: Vicarious reinforcement and imitative learning. *Journal of abnormal and social psychology,* 67, 1963, pp 601–607.

12 Bandura, A: Influence of model's reinforcement contingent on the acquisition of imitative responses. *Journal of personality and social psychology,* 1, 1965, pp 589–595.

13 Liebert, R M, and Baron, R A: Some immediate effects of televised violence on children's behaviour. *Developmental psychology,* 6, 1972, pp 469–475.

14 Drabman, R S, and Thomas, M H: Does media violence increase children's toleration of real-life aggression? *Developmental psychology*, 10, 1974, pp 418—421.

15 Bandura, A: What TV violence can do to your child. Pp 123—130 in Larsen, O N (ed): *Violence and the mass media*. New York: Harper and Row, 1968.

16 Fesbach, S, and Singer, R: *Television and aggression*. San Francisco: Jossey Bass, 1971.

17 Friedrich, L, and Stein, A H: Aggressive and prosocial television programs and the natural behavior of preschool children. *Monographs of the Society of Research in Child Development*, 38, 1973, (4, serial no 151).

18 Howitt, D, and Dembo, R: A subcultural account of media effects. *Human relations*, 27, 1974, pp 25—41.

Chapter 5

PROGRAMMES FOR CHILDREN

In this chapter and the one immediately following it we consider the influence of programmes that have been specially made for children. Some children's programmes are manufactured simply to entertain, while others are designed with a clear intention to instruct the young, but many, perhaps the majority of those shown on British television, are intended to combine entertainment and educational functions. Television materials intended primarily to instruct, including items such as the American *Sesame Street* series and British items for schools broadcasting, will be surveyed in the following chapter. The present one considers programmes for children that do not clearly belong to the instructional category, bearing in mind that no hard-and-fast dividing line exists.

Surprisingly little is known about the effects of British-made programmes for children. To this adult viewer, the standards of children's television seen on British television appear to be admirably high, and the viewing figures for both BBC and ITV late-afternoon transmissions suggest that the intended audience is well pleased by what is made available. One expects Westerns, spy thrillers and adventure series to be popular, but it is gratifying to discover that the kinds of programmes which an educated adult might regard as having more to contribute to growing minds, such as *Blue Peter, Jackanory, Play Away* and *Play School* also appear to be much-liked by large numbers of child viewers. Furthermore, a number of recent British-made series and serials that do contain the classic elements for gaining children's attention—adventure, excitement and suspense—have managed at the same time to incorporate considerable authentic human interest. They involve the lives of individuals for whom children can have empathy, emotions that are real, and a concern with the importance of qualities such as thoughtfulness, awareness and understanding lacking in the blander, stereotyped and often relatively mindless formula Westerns and thrillers to which we have grown accustomed.

107

This is not to deny that a number of offensive and trivial programmes are also regularly shown. Both the BBC and the independent channels also broadcast materials of low quality, some of the worst being in cartoon form. The BBC has its share of violent American-made cartoons (*Yogi Bear, Tom and Jerry*) and less violent ones, such as *Valley of the Dinosaurs* and *Astronut*. Cartoon violence on the independent channels is found in *The Woody Woodpecker Show*, and a weekend morning is likely to contain examples of both the best (*Sesame Street*) and the worst (*Tarzan*) imports from the United States. Nevertheless, a high proportion of the programmes that all British television channels make available for children are of high quality and are non-violent.

It is not always easy to produce materials that are both educationally valuable and also sufficiently attractive to a wide range of children to compete successfully for their attention with a Western or spy-thriller that may be showing on a rival channel. The outcomes of attempts to achieve both these goals can appear to suffer, at least from an adult standpoint, by being brash, glib and superficial. High quality programmes such as *Blue Peter* and *Play Away* sometimes reflect too obvious a desire on the part of their producers to keep things moving, by repeated changes in pace, presumably in an effort to avoid losing viewers' attention. Yet television producers do have good reasons for believing that the informative 'magazine' type of children's programme can only hold its viewers in competition with thrillers and adventure series if it contains large measures of zest, energy and obvious enthusiasm. Items tend to be quick, snappy and rather frequently changed, and if an adult does find the resulting mixture over-hearty and too bombastic for his taste, and lacking in depth, so much the worse for him. Sometimes it is useful to remind ourselves that children's programmes are for children.

The BBC has long been aware that if television is to hold children's attention it has to entertain them. Its producers have been rightly suspicious of the kind of worthy but dull programming that is liable to arise when earnest and well-meaning attempts to educate children and increase their knowledge are put into practice without enough emphasis on gaining attention, or sufficient willingness to meet the child at his own level of interest. The Independent Television Company's *Guide* for 1975 also stresses the attempts to keep a balance between entertainment and information, whereby material aimed at the child's intelligence is as entertaining as possible, while the stories, cartoons and comedies made to bring pleasure will also convey useful information. Of course, these dual aims are by no means always achieved.

108

The popularity of a programme for children is certainly no guarantee of its quality, nor of its ability to stimulate and engage the child at a non-superficial level, and thus extend his insight and understanding. But, as in the case of adult television, unless a significant number of viewers choose to watch a particular programme its value is minimal, however worthy its maker's intentions. Producers of television for children know that the late-afternoon period during which most children's weekday programmes are transmitted is a time when children have just returned home from a busy day at school. They are likely to be tired and more in need of relaxation, perhaps involving a certain amount of fantasy content, than of serious intellectual challenge.

In an earlier chapter we have shown that children are heavy consumers of television. While both the BBC and its independent rivals would prefer that as many children as possible choose their particular brand of television to the alternative channel, it is not the desire of the British television executives to increase the total number of hours the children spend watching. Indeed, one indication of the success of certain kinds of programmes is their effectiveness in directing children away from the screen to spend time in alternative activities that concern considerable involvement and participation—hobbies, sports, reading, music and other interests. Programmes such as *Blue Peter* frequently contain demonstrations and instructions for making things, and information about a variety of children's activities. Unfortunately, little detailed or systematic information exists concerning the effectiveness of such efforts to encourage young children to participate in these varied activities. An indication of their impact is the fact that the BBC reports that chidren send over 4000 letters each week to *Blue Peter,* some offering suggestions and others seeking information. (1) In addition, competitions are known to be very successful in getting large numbers of children busily engaged at activities such as designing posters, making models and composing limericks. One competition for a 'Keep Britain Tidy' poster drew 150,000 entries. Large numbers of children are also willing to collect items in order to aid the needy, and requests for scrap materials are likely to produce up to half a million contributions.

In the United States television for children has been retarded by the commercial domination of the American television industry. A marketplace philosophy exists, by which programmes are regarded as products for a market of viewers. This does little to promote the qualities required for good children's programming, such as imagination and inventiveness, and willingness to admit responsibility to do more than maintain the

109

child's attention by the easiest and cheapest means is noticeably absent. Advertising revenue is guaranteed by reliance upon formulas known to attract large number of child viewers. Such proven formulas very often contain action and conflict, as these facilitate the speedy build-up of the kind of plot that makes for an easily and cheaply produced package. (2) In order to attract as many viewers as possible, and thus persuade advertisers that they will make money by sponsoring a particular programme, efforts are made to avoid offending anyone. Consequently, shows are designed to be noncontroversial, and this places a further restriction on diversity and inventiveness. Another cause of the lack of variety lies in the fact that a small number of advertisers provide the major portion of the income for sponsoring children's programmes. Manufacturers of US programmes for distribution to child viewers via the commercial networks have displayed remarkably little interest in the special needs of children. The viewing ratings provide the source of feedback to which they give closest attention. Actual contacts between children or their parents and the makers of programmes are extremely restricted. (3) No research into the child audiences is undertaken, and even the practice of making pilot programmes, a standard procedure for series designed for adults, is omitted from children's programmes, since it costs money. The US networks each purchase a package of child series, and normally agree to rerun each episode either six times over two years or eight times over three years. Various spin-offs such as toys, records and books add to the financial attractiveness of popular items.

 Commercial pressures in the United States not only act to reduce the quality of children's television but also lead to the introduction of excessive amounts of advertising. In *Romper Room* for instance, an ostensibly 'educational' programme of poor quality, one viewing mother observed that during a typical half-hour show four and a half minutes contained straightforward commercials, six minutes were spent playing with the *Romper Room* toys that the commercials in the same show had advertised, and a further six minutes were used to play with other *Romper Room* toys. (4) This proportion of advertising material is much higher than would be permitted in adult programmes. In general, the quantity of advertising on United States children's television is around three times that allowed in Britain, and in most European countries the amount permitted is even less.

Whenever it is not commercially profitable, the sheer quantity of children's programming in America is likely to be small. In Chicago it was observed around 1960 that the three television networks contributed
110

between them a grand total of one hour of children's materials each weekday. Often the vast majority of children's items do not even aim to offer more than straight entertainment. For example, during 1970 it was reported that cartoons formed eighty-four per cent of the programmes for children transmitted in the Washington DC area. ✳

Knowing something about the effects of commercial domination on standards of television for children in the US might lead us to expect that children's materials made available by the commercial television companies in Britain would be substantially inferior to those transmitted by the BBC. As it happens, the BBC seems to outscore its commercial rivals in both the amount and quality of television broadcasting for children. Furthermore, children appear to have a slight preference for those items the BBC provides for them. There are some discrepancies between the viewing figures issued by the BBC and by the ITV companies, due to differing measurement techniques, but the weekday afternoon items during which children's programmes are continuously transmitted are among the few periods when BBC 1 programmes are regularly seen by considerably more children (according to BBC figures) or by as many children (according to ITV data) as are items presented on the commercial channels.

On a typical weekday afternoon in early Spring 1975, excluding schools broadcasts, the BBC 1 shows for children start with *Teddy Edward* at 1.50pm, an animated series predictably involving a bear. At 4.00 there is *Play School,* repeating a programme shown during the morning on BBC 2, and then follows a short Czechslovak cartoon film called *Dorothy,* about a small girl with a parrot. Next comes *Jackanory,* a programme that has proved highly popular over a number of years, in which stories are told. At 4.45 there is an American cartoon, relatively non-violent, called *Valley of the Dinosaurs.* This is followed by *John Craven's Newsround, Vision On,* and, finally, *Barbapapa,* an imaginative French cartoon series involving animals that can change in shape.

The commercial offerings (Westward Television) on the same afternoon are considerably more restricted. *Hickory House* at 12.00pm is followed by a two-minute local presentation, *Gus Honeybun's Birthdays.* There is nothing else for children until 4.25, when *The Sooty Show* is presented, and then *Magpie,* which completes the children's fare.

In the United States the aforementioned hindrances imposed by commercial domination of the medium have ensured that the general level of quality of children's programmes is low. Nevertheless, a few very good children's shows have appeared. Most of the better items have been distributed by publicly-financed stations, and the low budgets on which these

111

channels have been forced to operate, at least until very recently, have sometimes been only too apparent in the standards of production. For instance, in *Captain Kangaroo,* which was among the better US children's programmes in the late sixties and early seventies, one could detect a feeling of concern for children, but sharp restrictions on budgeting induced a certain absence of vitality and imagination.

An experimental study

In the pre-*Sesame Street* era of children's television in the USA, *Mister Rogers Neighborhood,* aimed at viewers around four years of age, was almost unique among children's shows in providing contents of a consistently high level. The programme combines two basic elements, one at a level of everyday reality, incorporating domestic scenes that involve Mister Rogers in his home. The other, at a fantasy level, involves a make-believe land ruled by King Friday the Thirteenth, and inhabited by puppets whose characters and temperaments are clearly defined and carefully developed. The transition between the 'real' world of Mister Rogers' home and the make-believe puppet land is handled with enormous delicacy and care, and the programme as a whole has a quiet low-key quality, apparently contradicting the usual lore concerning how to engage and maintain young children's attention. Mister Rogers is noticeably unaggressive, perhaps even passive by American standards. At the beginning of a show he is seen to enter the room shown on the screen. He changes into his indoor clothes and chats casually in a quiet voice to the child audience about themselves, their likes and dislikes, their feelings, fears, jealousies and concerns. Sometimes he talks to the children about problems they are likely to encounter at home, when they are naughty, for example, or when Mummy has to give much of her time and attention to a new baby, or about concern at going to the barber for a haircut. (He doesn't cut off anything except hair, Mister Rogers explains, and it always grows again.) Sometimes people from the 'Neighborhood' are brought in and introduced, the postman or a shopkeeper, for instance. Throughout there is an emphasis on acceptance of the child viewer as the individual he is. 'I like you as you are', says Mister Rogers in speech and song, and he reassures his child viewers that each of them is worth while in his own way, and that all of their feelings, of rage, jealousy and badness are as acceptable and as usual as those of loving and caring. In the world of make-believe the problems and conflicts encountered by the puppet characters have a direct bearing upon the children's own lives. Experiences of jealousy, love, caring for people, controlling angry feelings are among the themes introduced.

112

There is a quality of sincerity in Mister Rogers. Expressed in print, the idea of a television personality looking out from the screen and solemnly saying 'I like you as you are' may seem artificial and possibly ridiculous. Yet when Mister Rogers says it he means it, and the children know that he really cares. The programme has continued to hold large audiences despite being transmitted on public 'Educational' channels which most American parents do not often turn to, and despite its lack of some of the programme characteristics often deemed to be essential for maintaining children's attention—noise, action, animation and constant change.

The originator of *MisterRogers Neighborhood,* Fred Rogers, has written that the programme is 'more an adult-child relationship than a children's television show'. (5) Children, he says, need first of all to recognise their own feelings and to be able to express them. The adult-child relationship is vital because children will only express their feelings when they trust that a caring adult will treat them with respect. The real drama, Rogers considers, is going on *within* the child. Rogers speaks of the need to treat child viewers with the dignity they deserve, to communicate the feeling of care and to aim at the building of self-esteem and greater understanding in children.

Through his songs, clearly defined fantasy and straightforward dialogue Rogers encourages children to realise that their individual feelings are both mentionable and manageable. In one of his songs he asks 'What do you do with the mad that you feel; when you feel so mad you could bite', and he goes on to make some practical suggestions. This contrasts with what he regards as the commercial cartoon approach in which when you are angry at someone you knock him down or flatten him out, and the problem will go away. Rogers writes of hoping to portray an alternative tradition, which shows 'that two men struggling hard to work out their anger with each other is far more dramatic than gunfire', and in which human life is seen to have great value, each person being equally worthwhile.

MisterRogers Neighborhood stands apart from other American children's programmes in the attention given to understanding the physical, emotional and social aspects of development in the children to whom it communicates. Lengthy and regular consultation between producers and experts in child development has been the rule. An added reason for interest in *MisterRogers Neighborhood* is that its effects have been measured in one of the very few investigations that have attempted to look for socially valuable, or 'prosocial' outcomes of watching television. The research investigation in question is the one by Lynette Friedrich and Aletha Stein mentioned in the previous chapters. (6) Over a four week period these authors ensured that each of a number of young children saw twelve

113

programmes belonging to one of three categories. Some children watched programmes containing much aggression and violence—*Batman* and *Superman*. Others saw television shows that contained neither violence nor materials of positive social value. A third group of children watched twelve episodes of *MisterRogers Neighborhood*, three per week over the four week period. It needs to be mentioned that for most of the children these twelve hours of controlled viewing represented only a small fraction of their total viewing over the period. They also watched television at home for a total of around eighty hours during the four weeks. For this reason, any effects of the different experimental programme diets used in the experiment may considerably underestimate the total impact of the television medium on children in their normal lives. The ages of the children were between three-and-a-half and five-and-a-half years.

Friedrich and Stein used a number of separate measures of positively valued social behaviour. First, they looked for instances of 'Prosocial interpersonal behaviour'. This category included cooperative acts that were involved in interactions with other children in role playing or in any activity whereby the children's behaviour was directed towards a common goal. The use of mature social skills was also considered to demonstrate prosocial interpersonal behaviour. For example, tactics such as distracting another individual from the real purpose of one's own actions, and the ploy of saying to another child 'Show me what a big boy you are by doing this', provided scorable instances of interpersonal skills. Also acceptable were expressions of nurturance or sympathy, as expressed by offers of help, appraisal or protection to another child. Finally, demonstrations of the ability to make statements describing one's feelings or explaining one's behaviour were counted as prosocial interpersonal behaviours.

The second major category of positively valued social behaviours was 'Persistence'. This was considered to be demonstrated by a child's attempt to master various tasks, or by his involvement in activities that required making things, playing with materials or practising motor skills. A child was regarded as demonstrating persistence when he was seen to be fully engaged in a task over a period of one minute or more, without often looking away, and made repeated attempts to overcome any difficulties that were experienced. Signs of being able to do things independently that might normally require adult help or supervision were also considered to be evidence of persistence.

Thirdly, the observers rated the children for signs of ability to use 'Rules and self-control'. Examples of acceptable behaviours included
114

behaving spontaneously in accordance with roles in a situation where there was a choice of actions, and the spontaneous voluntary performance of mature activities such as cleaning-up, stating rules or asking questions about them, and voluntarily tolerating delays as when waiting for materials or for the help and attention of an adult.

The authors anticipated that the effects, if there were any, of the three experimental conditions would vary with the characteristics of the individual children. Therefore, for some analyses of the findings, the child subjects were divided by sex, by social class and intelligence, and according to their initial aggressiveness prior to seeing the television programmes. All of these were assessed during the three-week baseline period.

As Friedrich and Stein expected, many of the children did show increases in socially-valued behaviours as a result of watching *MisterRogers Neighborhood*. For the category of prosocial interpersonal actions, children in the lower half of the social-class distribution made statistically significant positive gains. Children from the lower social classes had considerable gains in the behaviours in this category during the experimental period, whereas comparable children in the alternative conditions did not. A possible reason for the social class difference in these effects of watching *MisterRogers Neighborhood* lies in the fact that middle-class children more frequently reported regularly viewing the programme at home. It may be that the *MisterRogers Neighborhood* episodes seen in the nursery school were more of a novelty to the others, and that the middle-class participants were not greatly influenced by what amounted to increased doses of something already being received.

Persistence at tasks was also influenced by the experimental conditions, and so were the social actions involved in self-regulation, such as obedience to rules and toleration of delays. In general, these behaviours declined among children who saw the aggressive programmes, whereas children who watched *MisterRogers Neighborhood* showed increases. The effects of the different programme diets were more pronounced among children who scored relatively high on intelligence tests than among the less intelligent. The children who watched *MisterRogers Neighborhood* not only acted more obediently to rules and increased in tolerance of delays during the experimental period, but persisted in doing so throughout the weeks afterwards. Among the more intelligent children, task persistence was especially strongly affected by *MisterRogers Neighborhood*. The authors of the study point out a contrast between the effects of *MisterRogers Neighborhood* on prosocial interpersonal behaviours and on the self-regulating actions. The former were most strongly influenced in children from lower social-class homes, whereas the latter showed larger changes among the more intelligent children. Since social class and intelligence were correlated, albeit weakly, it appears to be the case that the different 'messages' in the programme reached different groups of children. As Friedrich and Stein point out, it is noteworthy that a wide range of children have been found to profit from *MisterRogers Neighborhood*, since it has been suggested that the primary appeal of this programme is to children from middle-class backgrounds. The authors also draw attention to the fact that marked effects took place in task persistence, which is an important element of achievement motivation in young children and contributes markedly to success in a range of life's tasks.

A number of complications hinder full explanation of Friedrich's and Stein's findings. For example, there is the fact that in everyday life the many television programmes a viewer sees differ in a variety of ways. There is no way of being sure which particular qualities are responsible for any effects that occur. In the present study, the 'aggressive' shows not only differed from *MisterRogers Neighborhood* in the amount of aggression as such, but they were also more noisy, contained greater quantities of rapid action and speedier transitions between sequences. By contrast, *MisterRogers Neighborhood* has a rather slow, soothing pace. Another obstacle to identifying the precise causes of the present investigation's outcomes lies in the fact that the experiment yielded no clear evidence of any imitative responses such as were found in Bandura's laboratory experiments. Social learning theory, as advanced by Bandura, would also lead one to expect that measures of the children's attention to the programmes and information about their interests would help predict the effects of the programmes on their behaviour. In fact this was not the case. Friedrich and Stein suggest that if we want to understand more about the effects of seeing television frequently and over long periods, we need to know more than we do about the intervening steps between observation and subsequent behaviour, especially since these are often widely separated in time and context.

Despite these complexities a clear and simple message does emerge from the findings of this investigation. The experience of watching *MisterRogers Neighborhood*—and presumably watching other well-constructed and responsibly envisaged programmes designed for children—does help children in ways that are decidedly valuable. In the case of *MisterRogers Neighborhood* it is possible, even likely, that the materials also help achieve Rogers' aim to bring about improvements in attributes that can less easily be defined or measured in strictly behavioural terms—understanding, self-esteem and the like— in addition to those documented by Friedrich and Stein. Their findings provide clear evidence that responsibly designed television contents can have a variety of benign influences upon young children. The onus is upon those who make decisions about the nature of the programmes transmitted to the young to ensure that the medium is utilized in ways which ensure the maximum benefit for children in need.

Research in Britain
There have been few attempts to measure the effects of children's programmes in the United Kingdom. Greater emphasis has been placed upon responses to television shows, patterns of media use, attitudes to certain materials and children's likes and dislikes. One investigation examined some reactions to *Blue Peter*, a very popular BBC programme in 'magazine' format. It is aimed primarily at the sevens-to-tens, but attracts large audiences throughout the five-to-twelve-years age range. (7) The researchers took an edition of *Blue Peter* containing seven major items, varying in subject, length, pace and location (studio materials or externally-produced films). Each item involved at least one of the three adult 'presenters' appearing on *Blue Peter*, John, Valerie and Peter. The main object of the investigation was to compare the opinions of child viewers and adult production staffs about the most effective manner of ordering the different items. The author suggests that television producers tend to follow a policy of presenting the most intersting material at the beginning, in order to 'hook' the audience, who are said to suffer from 'button apathy'—a reluctance to switch channels, once a programme has begun. In reality it is somewhat doubtful whether this kind of reasoning has much force in the case of regularly viewed children's programmes such as *Blue Peter*. For a start, no child I have encountered has ever suffered from button apathy. Most youngsters have no hesitation in switching channels, at the drop of a hat, and the major problem is to restrain them from doing so. Secondly, the audience for a show such as *Blue Peter* are mainly regular viewers, who know perfectly well what kinds of content they can expect in the programme as a whole, irrespective of the opening sequence. Most children choose either to watch all the programme or not to view it at all.

The researcher who carried out this study decided to ask some children and some adult producers of the series for their views about the optimum order of presenting the different items. Children who had watched the

117

programme were shown several still photographs representing the items they had seen. Each child was asked to select the running order he would have chosen had be been in charge of production, and he was also asked why each part would have been placed in the position selected. The children varied considerably in their orders of preference, but the item most often chosen for first place was the one that had in fact appeared first, the one most often chosen second was the one that occurred second in the original programme, and so on. They tended to select short fast items to start with, and chose slow and relatively unexciting items for the later positions. However, since all the children had watched the programme with the items ordered identically, it is difficult to assess the significance of this finding. Quite possibly the respondents might have come to regard the order in which they had seen the items as being the most 'natural' one, and responded on that basis when asked to arrange the parts in order of preference. The author had previously found that children aged around six years were unable to comprehend the story-line of a puppet film. In the present study it was observed that some children of this age found items made outside the studio to be rather frightening. For example, in the case of a filmed traction engine there was concern that it might blow up. The younger children expressed some preference for the familiar environment shown in the studio sequences, and reported liking these parts because they found them safe. Older children tended to prefer items that were more unusual, and these were often materials made externally on film.

When the adult television producers were asked to choose a preferred arrangement of the items, they tended to select orderings based on their order of preference, starting with the item liked best and considered most important. Their arrangements were appreciably less varied than those of the children, and some of the items to which the producers responded enthusiastically were not positively liked by the child viewers. Most producers would have chosen to commence with an item recorded on film, whereas children tended to place such materials in the middle of the programme. The findings as a whole are consistent with the suggestion that producers and young children differ in that the former place emphasis on gaining and holding attention, whereas a child is more inclined to seek security. But the evidence is not sufficiently clearcut to provide firm support for such a generalization.

An interesting research project conducted in Europe took the form of a study of the reactions of child viewers in a number of different countries to a prize-winning children's programme. (1) The item in
118

question was *Patrik und Putrik,* a fifteen-minute puppet story, the winning entry in the Prix Jeunesse competition held in Munich during 1966. *Patrik und Putrik* shows two flexible puppets who try to bake some biscuits for themselves. In the course of their attempts they have a series of mishaps. The film, which is intended to be humorous, contains no language, and this was a major consideration underlying the choice of it as the subject of a research investigation that involved international cooperation.

The first finding of note was that, although the film had been selected by an adult jury as the prize-winner from a large number of entries, the children who were asked to watch it, aged between five and eight years, did not particularly like it. Different nationalities varied in their reactions to *Patrik und Putrik.* For instance the French children enjoyed it more than the British children, many of whom clearly disliked it. It was often rated as being considerably less enjoyable than the children's favourite programmes, but the low rating may have been due partly to its unfamiliarity. Differences in the precise form of the research procedures followed in the various countries make it disappointingly difficult to provide realistic comparisons. Children in Czechoslovakia tended to rate *Patrik und Putrik* more negatively than other nationalities, a possible explanation being that Czechoslovakian experience with puppets leads to higher standards of puppet appreciation and higher expectancies than are found in participants from other nations. In most of the countries respondents stressed the comical nature of the programme when asked what they liked about it, but the nationalities differed with respect to the particular contents they found most amusing.

Unfortunately the responses were not patterned in a systematic manner that might have suggested broad generalizations about national differences in humour. The German researchers referred to identification as being a major factor, and in support of this assertion they mention that child viewers especially liked the scenes in which the characters' activities corresponded with things they would like to undertake themselves. Among the French children it was found that incidents intended to be humorous were not regarded as being so if they caused hurt or produced major breaks in the film sequence. The French researchers considered that some of the children attributed to the programme a logicality that was in fact lacking from it. The suggestion that children may have done so accords with the British psychologist Sir Frederick Bartlett's statement that a common response of the human learner to relatively unfamiliar information takes the form of an 'effort after meaning', by which the learner searches for ways of interpreting the new material in terms of a familiar frame of reference. The French children's comments show greater sophistication than those of other nationalities, and were more serious, more articulate and more inclined to moralize. However, it is quite likely that the French sample contained a larger proportion of middle-class children than the other groups, and the authors point out that practical difficulties made it impossible for all the participating countries to keep to an agreed sampling plan. Categorization by social class in empirical research of this nature, whilst straightforward enough in countries like Britain and the United States, is beset with problems in nations where research traditions are dissimilar or where substantially different political and social philosophies apply, as in Czechoslovakia.

It is a pity that the high standards of materials for children shown on British television have not been matched by well-constructed research studies designed to assess their influence. We know very little about what British children actually learn from the programmes designed for them or about the manner and extent to which attitudes and behaviour are affected by children's television. Research—most of it American— has shown very convincingly that television can and does influence children in a number of ways, including ones that are socially desirable, and it therefore forms a powerful and important agent of socialization in their lives. Those programmes which are intended to have positive and desirable effects, so far as child viewers are concerned, ought to attract at least as much attention, in the form of investigations examining their outcomes, as do television contents which we believe may have damaging influences upon our children.

A number of American investigations have considered the effects of television contents that have been designed with explicit learning outcomes in mind. The aims of such programmes have most often been to promote the growth of intellectual skills and knowledge, rather than to bring about learning with a strong social or emotional component. There have been a number of attempts to carefully measure outcomes of educational materials, at least as far as knowledge is concerned. Even here a discrepancy exists, in that while Britain has produced a greater volume of apparently good educational material for children than has the United States, in the latter country there has been greater emphasis on systematic and careful evaluation of the materials that are available. Programmes specifically designed to help children learn are considered in the following chapter.

120

REFERENCES

1 *Children as viewers and listeners.* London: BBC, 1974.

2 Melody, W: *The unique characteristics of children's television.* New Haven, Connecticut: Yale University Press, 1973.

3 Leifer, A D, Gordon, N J, and Graves, S B: Children's television: more than entertainment. *Harvard educational review,* 44, 1974, pp 213–245.

4 Sarson, E: Growing grass roots in viewerland. *Television quarterly,* 9, 1970, pp 50–58.

5 Rogers, F M: Television and individual growth. *Television quarterly,* 9, 1970, pp 14–19.

6 Friedrich, L and Stein, A H: Aggressive and prosocial television programs and the natural behavior of preschool children. *Monographs of the Society for Research in Child Development,* 38, 1973, (4, serial no 151).

7 Noble, G: Concepts of order and balance in a children's TV program. *Journalism quarterly,* 47, 1970, pp 101–108, 159.

Chapter 6

TELEVISION TO HELP CHILDREN LEARN

In Britain today it is widely accepted that television has a role in helping children acquire knowledge and skills contributing to their education. Figures issued in 1974 show that television materials made available by schools' broadcasting services were used by eighty-four per cent of all primary schools and sixty-four per cent of secondary schools. (1) The fact that the schools make extensive and regular use of the materials that are made available for them provides one indication of television's effectiveness. However, as was true in the case of the British television programmes mentioned in the previous chapter, our knowledge of the manner in which children are influenced by the schools programmes is patchy and incomplete. Some research has been undertaken, but it has tended to be informal and to concentrate on the verbal reactions of teachers to what their pupils see. Annual surveys provide detailed figures concerning audience sizes, but as yet there exists little systematically-obtained quantitative evidence to show the actual impact of these programmes upon their intended audience.

For detailed knowledge about the effectiveness of television programmes designed to help children learn we have to look at research conducted in the United States. There, the current state of affairs in children's educational television parallels the situation encountered in the previous chapter, in connection with general programming for children. High-quality educational programmes for children have been few in number, but the best have been very good indeed. Most importantly, and most noticeably in the case of *Sesame Street,* there have been instances, unparalleled in the United Kingdom, of extensive collaboration between television producers and experts on human learning and child development. In addition to the cooperation in designing evaluation studies, through which it has been possible to find out how viewers were affected by the programmes they have seen, researchers and producers have worked together in the initial planning of programmes.

122

This close cooperation between broadcasters and child researchers has been the most significant feature of *Sesame Street*. It has led to the production of a television programme in which the contents are closely based upon knowledge of what young children need to know and about their manner of learning, and also to the acquisition of detailed feedback about the effectiveness of the materials produced as a result of this cooperation. Detailed feedback is essential if one wishes to discard or modify television items that do not meet their intended aims. In the present chapter we first discuss *Sesame Street* and some other recent American experiments. Afterwards, schools' television services in Britain are briefly surveyed.

Sesame Street

Circumstances in Britain, whereby schools' television services produced by the BBC and by companies under the Independent Television Authority function on a national basis, in collaboration with the schools, are not paralleled in the United States. There is no provision of a public radio system broadcasting to schools there, and educational television for use in schools has mainly been on a small-scale and local basis, often hampered by financial restrictions and by a lack of the professional skills and the equipment necessary for high production standards. In contrast to most educational programmes in Britain, *Sesame Street*, which is aimed primarily at pre-schoolers, was made by individuals working quite outside the formal educational system. Nevertheless, Martin Meyer's judgement that *Sesame Street* is 'by any standards the largest educational experiment ever', (1) is probably correct.

Sesame Street was originally envisaged in the mid-1960s and it got off the ground largely through the efforts of Mrs Joan Ganz Cooney, a television producer, who was able to gain the financial support of the Carnegie Corporation and the Ford Foundation. (2) It took some years for the programme to be developed. Initially, a number of ideas were expressed about ways to make use of the wasted educational opportunities of the medium, especially in the pre-school years, and it was suggested that stories and conversation involving child and adult performers, might be used, and also puppets. At a later stage the idea of having cartoons was introduced, with commercial-like formats to sell young children 'things they ought to know'. It was decided to have an old district in a large city as the permanent set, in which a group of residents would provide the 'hosts' for the show and give day-to-day continuity. 'Sesame' in the title was taken from Ali Baba's 'Open Sesame' in *The thousand and one nights*.

123

By 1968 some basic goals of *Sesame Street* had been established. Each of these had the quality of being definable in terms of specific child behaviours, and fell into one of four major categories. These are 'Symbolic representation', 'Cognitive organization', 'Reasoning and problem solving' and 'The child and his world'. The abilities involved in symbolic representation include knowledge of letters, numbers and some simple words and geometric forms. Cognitive processing in children includes skills based upon perceptual discrimination, knowledge of relationships, classification and ordering. Reasoning and problem-solving capacities include the ability to infer antecedent events and to predict subsequent developments, and to put forward explanations and evaluate them. The concepts taught in *Sesame Street* that relate to the child and his world include recognition of the parts of the body, and an elementary understanding of social groups and social interactions.

An hour's show on *Sesame Street* is likely to contain between thirty and fifty separate parts, the total time being divided roughly equally between the above four categories. A team of educational psychologists makes up a list of the specific targets for a particular day, and this specifies the letters and numbers to receive special attention, and the concepts to be taught. (3) A large amount of repetition is allowed between programmes, only about half of every hour-long show being produced solely for that day.

The idea of having close collaboration between television producers and researchers met with a good deal of initial suspicion, even scepticism. Television producers are inclined to proceed on the basis of their intuitions about what will appeal to an audience. Researchers in child learning and development like to state clear goals for an educational experiment but they are liable to speak in somewhat abstract and global terms. At first the production teams were constantly asking 'What do you mean?' when faced with terms such as 'cognitive process' that are familiar to scientific researchers. It was necessary for statements about aims to be stated in terms that specified precise behavioural objectives. What the producers and writers required from the researchers were sets of desired educational outcomes that were sufficiently concrete and detailed to be readily translated into actual television programming. Therefore, precise descriptions were provided specifying what a child would be able to do when he had mastered each skill. To help the production staff translate the desired goals into actual scripts that described characters' actions and dialogue, the researchers provided a 'Writers' manual'. This listed a range of situations which are familiar to young children, and gave advice
124

about various teaching strategies which can be used. For example, the information provided in the guide to clarify the meaning of one goal—the ability to take another person's point of view—and to suggest how producers might teach children some of the component abilities, included precise behavioural objectives for the goal. One was that a child should recognize that a single event may be seen and interpreted in more than one way by different individuals. A child can be seen to appreciate this if, when handed a picture showing one boy in a bathing suit and another boy in a snowsuit, he is able to express the different feelings of the two boys in the event of snow. In addition to precisely specifying desired behaviours, the authors of the guide drew attention to some possible teaching strategies. For example, they suggested that the child's own point of view might be presented at first, followed by the opposing point of view. A second suggestion was to ask the child to pretend that he was someone else, who clearly had a different viewpoint from his own. Thirdly, a two-person situation could be devised, in which one individual was completely oblivious of the other's different point of view, demonstrating the need for communication. A fourth concrete suggestion was to show one constant situation and have a number of characters come in and react to it in very different ways.

It is not easy to bring about successful cooperation between broadcasters and researchers, since their skills and approaches are likely to be very different. There are a number of pitfalls and it is difficult to create programmes that incorporate the detailed and analytical approach necessary for meeting particular instructional goals, without destroying the vivacity and apparent spontaneity that is essential if a television show is to entertain its audience. However, *Sesame Street* has very convincingly shown that such cooperation can be successful, even on a large scale.

It should be emphasised that the aim of *Sesame Street* has been to teach a limited number of skills which are valuable for all young children. As initially conceived, *Sesame Street* aimed to be particularly helpful to those children, many of whom live in ghetto areas of large cities, who are regarded as 'disadvantaged' or deprived of some of the things that tend to be taken for granted in middle-class neighbourhoods—relative stability, considerable parent-child interaction, the availability of books and games in the home, and good nursery schools. However, the *Sesame Street* production team eventually decided against catering for children with particular 'deficits' in their previous learning. The decision was made to teach only the skills and knowledge that are likely to be useful for all children, in understanding their lives and coping with their environments. There was some emphasis on abilities necessary for getting the most out of education at school when the child arrived there, such as knowledge of letters and numbers.

Considerable thought was given to making the most effective use of the television medium. The fact that television reaches a mass audience provides a reason for concentrating upon those kinds of learning which are valuable to all, rather than upon minority interests. Since children's actions cannot be controlled by a television set in the way that they can by a teachers, the material needs to be entertaining; otherwise it is unlikely to maintain a child's constant attention. The circumstances of home viewing make the medium unsuitable for providing closely sequenced instruction in the way that is done at school. Considerations such as these encouraged the designers of *Sesame Street* to insist that the instructional capabilities of television are not unlimited. Television cannot replace and ought not to compete with the other agencies that promote learning in the young.

Sesame Street very definitely aims to entertain, and from its conception the makers have had little time for the view that education and entertainment are incompatible. In addition to the extensive use of animation and various audience-holding techniques that are borrowed from commercial television, *Sesame Street* draws upon a range of puppets who portray a variety of distinctive personalities. These puppets, developed from James Henson's 'Muppets', remain reliably in character over a range of episodes, and have proved enormously popular. One of their advantages is that they enable the portrayal of roles and functions that are more exaggerated and therefore clearer to children than is possible when live human characters are used. Among the puppet characters, as any child who watches *Sesame Street* knows, are the Cookie Monster, who is voracious and sly, devoting his life to hatching plots for deceiving others into satisfying his insatiable appetite for bicuits, and Oscar (The Grouch) who is strongly and reliably contrary in every respect, thriving on disorder, dirt and surliness, and choosing to despise the usual virtues of friendliness, cleanliness, consideration for others and gregariousness. Big Bird is flustered and confused, making mistakes all the time. Kermit the Frog is a gentlemanly young character who gets into all kinds of trouble but tries to stay cool and calm. Ernie is a crafty tease who usually appears with his long-suffering straight-man Bert. These and a variety of other puppets all have recognizable personalities which the child viewers can get to know, and the fact that their actions become partly predictable to the audience is an important element in their attractiveness.

126

Sesame Street makes use of a fair number of teaching procedures and devices. Some are based upon familiar teaching lore. For example, it is known that children often learn most effectively when the teacher starts from a basis of what is already highly familiar to them, and extends knowledge by building a bridge to facts and concepts that are new and unfamiliar. An illustration of such bridge-building in *Sesame Street* is encountered in a sequence about the letter 'J'. Two boys are seen watching a large J descend from above them, and one boy remarks that it looks like a fishhook. The narrator is heard to say 'It's not a fishhook, it's a J'. There follows a sequence in which the letter is used in a short story that contains numerous J sounds and words that begin with J. As the story ends, one of the boys says 'So that's the letter J', and the other replies 'It still looks like a fishhook to me!'.

Other teaching procedures used in *Sesame Street* draw more closely upon the particular qualities of the television medium. An example is a sequence intended to teach children to discriminate between the letters E and F, which they sometimes confuse. Big Bird, the easily flustered tall feathered puppet (with a man inside) is shown drawing an E and an F on the blackboard. After the letters have been completed the bottom line of the E migrates on its own to the F, so that the former E becomes an F and the F turns into an E. As the line begins, magically, to move, viewers hear the sound of a slide whistle, providing an additional cue that something odd is happening. It was observed that without the whistle children stop attending to this sequence after Big Bird has completed his task. The added auditory element contributes markedly to maintaining children's attention and directing it.

Some of the information that is presented on *Sesame Street* is designed primarily to show to the child certain aspects of the world he inhabits, and to guide him through some of the difficulties of modern urban life. Among the locations that have been visited are a car assembly plant, a fishing boat, a bakery, a farm, several zoos and an African play area for children. One film took children on a bus ride around town, and showed the driver performing his various tasks and interacting with the passengers. Apart from illustrating the physical world, it is intended that the adult actors in films of this kind will provide models for the children's behaviour. The child can watch people treating each other with decency and consideration, and, it is hoped, learn to act in similar ways. A belief of the makers of *Sesame Street* is that it is more effective to show adult models engaged in desirable behaviours that the children can imitate than to lecture to children or preach to them about how they ought to behave. In addition,

127

talking down to child viewers, or speaking to them in a special 'talking to children' voice, is definitely taboo.

A variety of devices are used for catching viewers' attention. Techniques encountered in commercial advertisements—animation, providing music and other sound effects—are much in evidence. Attractive and realistic settings are considered essential, as is the use of skilled professional actors. There is nothing amateurish about *Sesame Street;* its designers have been fully aware that no educational programme will win an audience solely by its good intentions. It is necessary to compete successfully with alternative television shows in which large sums of money have been spent on achieving high technical standards.

Music is used in a number of ways. It serves as a memory aid for learning relatively lengthy materials, for example the alphabet, which children can easily learn to sing. Rhythmic patterns and music are also used to facilitate learning of other sequenced items, such as the twelve months of the year or the days in a week. Music is provided to signal the arrival of familiar contents or characters. The show included a number of songs, these are often very popular with children, and records containing them are purchased in large numbers. It has been noticed that the songs in *Sesame Street* often evoke considerable physical participation. Younger children tend to rock and sway in response, and older ones sometimes get up and dance, especially if the song has a bouncy melody. Care is taken to integrate musical materials and sound effects with the visual content of an episode, since music does not engage a young child's attention if it is associated with static visual items, such as a stationary folk-singer or a seated orchestra. It is much more effective when it is closely integrated with exciting visual materials.

Repetition provides a further device for ensuring viewers' attention. Young children like part of what they watch to be familiar to them, and repeated presentation of content that is initially difficult or incompletely understood enables a child to gain increasing mastery. One use of repetition that is common on *Sesame Street* involves keeping the central material constant whilst altering the contexts in which it appears. For example, recognition of the letter 'N' is taught in three animated films and in a number of incidents involving live characters. Sometimes N appears as a line drawing, sometimes as a cardboard cut-out and sometimes as a three-dimensional object. Always, however, despite the changed formats, the N retains its distinctive features, helping the child learn that the letter he has learned remains constant despite the various alterations in the circumstances of its appearance.

128

Other devices that are used to maintain viewers' attention and interest include the classic elements of suspense and incongruity. These can encourage a child to confront the problems posed by deviations from his expectations. A jumping horse is suddenly stopped in mid-air, or water flowing in a stream is suddenly stopped and begins to flow backwards. Children also enjoy seeing adults making errors, destroying the myth of adult infallibility. A number of sequences with 'Buddy and Jim' show the two male adult characters having all kinds of trouble as they attempt apparently simple tasks, such as getting an ironing board through a door, making a sandwich, or putting a picture on the wall. Humour, much of it slapstick, is present in many *Sesame Street* items. As well as amusing the young audience, humour serves to engage the interest of adults and older brothers and sisters. Nothing is specifically designed for older viewers, but the makers of *Sesame Street* are happy when parents and others watch with the young children for whom the programme has been designed.

The sheer diversity of the different elements of *Sesame Street* makes it difficult to provide a short and neat summary of the show's typical contents. An easily apparent feature of *Sesame Street* is its use of a large number of short sequences, very few of which are over three minutes in length. Humour is one quality which many, if not most, of the widely varying parts possess in common. Much of *Sesame Street*'s attractiveness to children lies in the variety of the techniques and devices that are drawn upon, and in the high quality of professionalism attained in the production process.

Over a period of several years, *Sesame Street* has attracted the prolonged and regular attention of large numbers of child viewers. But this alone is not the proof of the pudding, so to speak. The huge financial investment in *Sesame Street* would be hard to justify unless it can be shown that it does succeed in meeting at least some of its intended goals. The question is, do children learn from *Sesame Street*? Are children who have watched the programme more successful than others at tasks designed to assess competence at what is taught in the programme?

The researchers who have had the task of evaluating *Sesame Street* have possessed a decided advantage over most investigators undertaking research into the effects of television. (4, 5) Planning for well-controlled evaluations of *Sesame Street* has proceeded, right from the outset, hand in hand with the designing of the programme itself. Added to this is the fact that the careful definition of goals in terms of precise child behaviours, not only facilitated the process of translation between the researchers' intentions

129

and the writers' productions but has made measurement of the programme's effects upon its viewers much more straightforward than is
usually the case.

It was considered important to look for unintended outcomes of
Sesame Street in addition to the ones which were anticipated. Concentrating only on intended functions and failing to look for unexpected
effects can lead to misleading conclusions, a fact which has been vividly
illustrated by the thalidomide case. In addition, there has been emphasis upon the importance of examining interactions between factors
rather than simply concentrating upon main effects. In other words, it
was considered necessary not only to discover whether seeing *Sesame
Street* affected the tested sample of children as a whole, but also to find
out which children learned most from it, for which individuals it was
least effective, and whether the show's impact was affected by
viewing conditions. *Sesame Street* may be more helpful to some young
children than to others, and if this is so it is important to know who is
helped most, and, if possible, why.

Field-interviewers were trained to administer a large battery of tests
to three- four- and five-year-olds, before and after exposure to *Sesame
Street*. The tests measured performance at thirty-six primary goals, and
also assessed other effects of the programme. A number of additional
measures were obtained, including information about home backgrounds,
parental attitudes and social class. Devices were built in to the battery
of tests to make it possible to detect misuse of them or dishonesty on
the part of the testers. The data from four out of the forty-odd testers
had to be discarded, causing loss of data from about ten per cent of the
subjects. The field-interviewers who did the testing were members of the
communities in which the children lived, and this fact probably contributed to the high level of cooperation by parents. Only about five per
cent refused the request to take part in the *Sesame Street* evaluation.

About 1300 children were initially tested. They came from a variety
of home environments, including large-city negro ghetto areas, middle
class suburbia, lower-class districts of a southern US town, poor rural
locations and Spanish-speaking homes. Some of the participants attended
nursery schools. Care was given to the design of tests permitting the child
viewers' responses to be scored easily and reliably. The eventual battery
contained over two hundred items, and required two hours of testing,
administered over three or four separate sessions. For most of the items,
simple pointing was the only overt response to be performed by the
child, and the staff who administered the tests received two days of
130

training. The numerous test items included questions covering a wide range of abilities, including naming parts of the body and stating their functions, recognizing naming and matching letters, specifying the initial sounds of words and reading simple words, recognizing and naming simple geometric forms, recognizing and naming numbers, and counting, addition and subtraction; matching; making proper use of relational terms referring to amount, size and position; sorting; classifying by size, form, number and function; perceiving incongruities; spotting embedded figures, and demonstrating an understanding of sequencing.

The unexpected popularity of *Sesame Street* raised problems for its evaluators. Originally, the plan was to compare performance by children who had watched the show and those who had not seen it. However, it turned out that only one eighth of the tested sample did not see the programme at all. Therefore, rather than comparing test-performance by viewers of *Sesame Street* with that of non-viewers, the *amount* of viewing was chosen as the variable which received attention in the bulk of the test-score analyses. The children were divided into four groups according to how often they had seen the show. A first group contained individuals who watched *Sesame Street* rarely or never, groups Two and Three included children who had intermediate amounts of exposure to the programme and those who saw it more than five times per week formed the fourth group.

Among the children as a whole, those who saw *Sesame Street* most often tended to perform best both on the pre-test administered before the show commenced and the post-test given after the first six months. They also showed the highest gains between pre-test and post-test. Thus it appears that the children who watched most often were both initially the most able and improved most from viewing *Sesame Street*.

The majority of the children who were tested came from backgrounds that could be loosely described as 'disadvantaged'. These individuals tended to watch slightly less than the average for the whole sample. Gains by the disadvantaged participants, like those of the sample as a whole, were directly related to the amount of time spent watching *Sesame Street*. Between pre-test and post-test the children who saw *Sesame Street* increased their test scores by an average of 18 points, advancing about 25 per cent from 75 to 93 points out of a possible score of 303. Part of this increase may have been due to increasing age, or to a test-retest effect, whereby having attempted a test on one occasion can lead to increased scores on the second administration of it. The disadvantaged children who watched *Sesame Street* most often gained considerably more points than the others. The group of them who watched most gained 47 points, an increase of approximately fifty per cent. Analyses in which the data was divided according to age show that the amount of viewing did not greatly vary with age, but that test scores and gains did. On the whole, the younger children had larger increases in their test scores after watching *Sesame Street,* the biggest improvements occurring among the three-year-olds. However, children of different ages varied in the particular abilities they acquired. Among those who watched *Sesame Street* most frequently, the three-year-olds made the largest gains in the tests relating to parts of the body, four-year-olds gained more than children of other ages in number skills, and five-year-olds showed the largest improvements in reading tests (a measure of transfer of learning, since reading words was not taught in the programme). It is interesting to note whereas most of the three-year-olds who watched *Sesame Street* frequently started with lower pre-test scores than any of the four- or five-year-old groups, their post-test scores, six months later, were higher than those of all the four-year-olds except the subgroup who viewed most, and higher than those of the two five-year-old groups who watched the show less frequently.

Among the disadvantaged children there were no major differences between boys and girls in the effects of *Sesame Street.* The two sexes spent an approximately equal amount of time watching the programme. Girls scored slightly higher at the pre-test, and on some items they gained a little more, as assessed by the difference between pre-test and post-test scores.

Disadvantaged children who received some form of nursery schooling scored higher on the pre-test than disadvantaged children at home all day. However, those children at home who did watch the programme gained more than most other subgroups. Children who attended nursery schools and saw *Sesame Street* at school increased their scores by roughly the same amount as other groups.

About one hundred and seventy of the participants came from middle-class homes in suburban Philadelphia. On the whole they watched *Sesame Street* more often than other children. Those among them who viewed most showed the largest gains in test scores, paralleling the findings for the total sample. However, in contrast with the results for the disadvantaged groups, the largest difference found within the middle-class children was between those who watched least and the group among the four who watched next least. Unlike the disadvantaged group, middle-class children who saw the programme most frequently did not gain much more than the children in the same group who watched infrequently. In the
132

post-test, middle class children who had watched little or none of the show received lower scores than heavy-viewing disadvantaged individuals, a fact which encouraged the authors of the evaluation study to suggest that *Sesame Street* can help to close the gap between advantaged and disadvantaged young children.

A small number of the children in the study came from families in which Spanish was the primary spoken language. Most of these children watched *Sesame Street* rather infrequently, but those of them who were heavy viewers of the programme made some extremely large gains, following very low pre-test scores. These large improvements were observed across a wide range of tests, suggesting that watching *Sesame Street* can be an especially valuable experience for children from non-English-speaking home backgrounds.

Another small sub-sample came from rural home environments, in North Eastern California. They tended to watch television less than the average for the total sample, but gained slightly more than other children who spent comparable amounts of time viewing. Again, those who viewed the most gained the most.

A number of more detailed analyses of the data were undertaken, to provide a closer examination of the impact of *Sesame Street*. For example, among children who viewed the programme extensively, an attempt was made to locate any differences between those who made large gains and those who improved least. No differences in intelligence were found between these two groups, but it was observed that the mothers of the children who learned most from the programme talked with their children about *Sesame Street* to a greater extent than did the other mothers. The mothers of the high gainers were slightly better educated, on average, and slightly more affluent than the others, and they were also more optimistic about their children's schooling.

In conclusion, *Sesame Street* has been shown to be a highly effective educational programme which has successfully taught basic skills to children from a range of very different home backgrounds. Most of the large gains occurred in areas that were taught directly, such as knowledge of letters, numbers, forms and body parts, sorting, classifying and use of relational terms. There was some evidence of transfer of learning to further intellectual skills, for example, to word identification among five-year-olds. However, there were few indications of other side-effects. Children aged three, four and five years old all benefited, but the five-year-olds tended to improve their levels of performance slightly less than the youngest children.

133

Sesame Street's great popularity among the children for whom it was designed to help ensures that a large number of those children who can benefit actually do see the programme. If there have ever been any real doubts that television can serve extremely well as a teaching medium, the findings of the evaluation study of *Sesame Street* clearly remove them. Of course, the aims of *Sesame Street* are by no means unlimited, a point often forgotten by some critics, who have castigated the programme for not increasing the growth of a variety of additional qualities which it has never been designed to promote. But *Sesame Street*'s success in achieving its goals among children from a variety of backgrounds should encourage those who are interested in the possibility of using the medium of television to communicate additional kinds of experience and to teach other abilities which are important in the lives of young children.

Further American research

The interest aroused by *Sesame Street* and the demonstration of its effectiveness have encouraged others to undertake experiments incorporating television as a learning medium for young children. One kind of enterprise has involved adapting *Sesame Street* materials to the needs of audiences different from the children for whom the programme was developed. A study was undertaken in Mexico City, to measure the effects of *Plaza Sesamo* (6), a Spanish-language version of *Sesame Street*. Experimental and control goups of children consisted of children attending day-care centres at the time when *Plaza Sesamo* was first broadcast, and the researchers were able to exert much closer control over the amount of time children spent watching the programme than was possible in the original evaluation of *Sesame Street*. Children in an experimental group, aged three, four and five, watched *Plaza Sesamo* at their day-care centre for fifty minutes each day, five days per week, over a period of six months. During this period the children who formed the control group saw cartoons and other non-educational television programmes. Two hundred and seventy children were involved in the study, and the three day-care centres which they attended catered mainly for children from the lowest social class, in which the head of the family had not completed primary education and was employed as an unskilled worker.

The investigators made strenuous efforts to ensure that whilst children in the experimental group saw *Plaza Sesamo* on as many weekdays as possible over the six-month period, the control groups watched it very infrequently, if at all. The research staff managed to persuade the day-care personnel and the administrative authorities to take the unusual step of

134

keeping the centres open over the four-day Easter Vacation period. Furthermore, the authorities were also persuaded to keep the centres open throughout a second vacation period, during May, lasting for eleven days. On this occasion it was anticipated that many parents would not send their offspring to the centres, even if they were open. Therefore, as a special inducement, the principal investigator offered his personal colour television set as a prize, to be raffled off among the parents of all the children attending the centres for every day over this the period of the vacation. Colour televisions are highly prized amongst the poor in Mexico City, and attendance during these eleven days turned out to be the highest for the entire six-month period. The report notes that the winner of the set, the father of one of the children in the control group, 'appeared the next day in his best attire, posing happily with his wife and child for photographs and basking in his enviable new status as the proud possessor of a color TV set'. (6)

The evaluation of *Plaza Sesamo* included a number of tests, most of which were translations or adaptations of measures developed for the evaluation of *Sesame Street*. The tests covered nine categories of abilities, general knowledge (eg, parts of the body), numbers, relations, embedded figures, parts of the whole, ability to sort, knowledge of letters and words, classification skills and oral comprehension. The largest differences between viewers and non-viewers were found among the four-year-olds, and the smallest in the three-year-olds. There were statistically significant differences between groups in test-score gains between pre- and post-tests, favouring the children who had watched *Plaza Sesamo*. Differences in gains were not only observed in those tests which dealt with content directly taught in the programme, such as general knowledge and letters, but also in the tests measuring abilities somewhat indirectly related to the contents of the programme. There were some large differences in learning between the experimental and control groups. For example, on the tests of letters and words both groups scored an average of 8.6 points in the initial pre-test, but six months later the experimental group averaged 14.4, an increase of about seventy per cent, whereas the average control group score was 10.2, the improvement being less than twenty per cent. The inter-group differences on a range of more broadly-based cognitive tests were not quite as striking as those for items specifically taught in *Plaza Sesamo*, but in each of the five general cognitive tests at least one of the three age groups showed significantly higher gains among viewers than among the control group. On a test of oral comprehension, which the authors report as being completely unrelated to the contents of the

135

programme, experimental-group children of all three ages made larger improvements than children who did not watch the show. The authors suggest that the gains between pre- and post-tests in this ability and those on the other cognitive tests that were not closely related to the contents of the television programme indicate that the experience of watching *Plaza Sesamo* may have yielded broad gains of a cognitive nature. Certainly, the children tested in this study manifested a range of side-effects not found among the viewers tested in the *Sesame Street* evaluation. The *Plaza Sesamo* findings indicate the possibility of improvements taking place across a range of the capacities that contribute to performance in tests of general intelligence.

One of the results of the *Sesame Street* study indicated that programmes like it might be especially valuable for children whose first language is not English, but who have to live in an English-speaking country, such as the United States. A television series called *Carrascolendas* was designed to meet the needs of Mexican-American children who inhabit a bicultural and bilingual environment. (7) *Carrascolendas* aims to help children acquire and use language skills in both Spanish and English, and also to improve performance at some of the cognitive and conceptual abilities taught in *Sesame Street,* including counting, number recognition, recognizing items in the physical environment and ability to discriminate. A series of thirty half-hour programmes have been developed, and as in *Sesame Street,* most of the individual segments contributing to each programme are short, ranging in length from twenty seconds to six minutes. Each segment has been designed to promote a carefully specified objective. Roughly equal numbers of English and Spanish language segments are included.

In general, the programme format is not unlike that of *Sesame Street,* using songs and puppets, and including some sequences of direct instruction. The set providing continuity for the series depicts a mythical Texan town inhabited by a number of characters including Senorita Barrera and Senor Vellareal, who often introduces and closes the programme, Mr Jones, the owner of a hamburger stand, Don Pedro, a young girl named Marieta, and Agapito, mischievous lion. A notable attribute of all the *Carrascolendas* characters, with the sole exception of Mr Jones, is that they speak in both Spanish and English.

To evaluate the series, eighty-eight school children aged six and seven years were randomly assigned to roughly equal groups of viewers and non-viewers. Prior to the transmission of *Carrascolendas* each child was given two pre-test interviews, one in English and one in Spanish. Post-tests in both languages were similarly administered about ten weeks later after

136

the thirty 30-minute programmes had been broadcast at the rate of three each week. It was considered important to provide an interesting alternative activity for the children who served as a control group, in order to avoid negative reactions by those not able to watch the programmes. The children forming the control group participated in a photography project that was specially designed for them.

Analysis of the test data showed that for the items tested in English there was a statistically significant overall difference between the groups. Children who watched *Carrascolendas* had larger increases in scores between pre- and post-tests. Yet there were no differences between the groups on the items tested in Spanish. Differences in specific English-language sub-tests were found in those items which related to social and physical environment, in the cognitive development tests measuring size and differences in temperature and weight. In two of the sub-tests, those relating to language skills and to numbers and figures, the experimental and control groups did not significantly differ. Children who had seen the programme also scored significantly higher than the others on ratings of ability to speak fluently and consistently in a single language.

The researchers who undertook the evaluation of *Carrascolendas* admit to being unsure why the Spanish-language tests did not reveal group-related differences in gains similar to those observed on items for which English was the language used in testing. They draw attention to the greater fluency in the post-test situation that was found in the children who watched the programme. A series such as *Carrascolendas* can be regarded as providing a useful supplement to the *Sesame Street* kind of approach. The latter attempts to help children from most if not all kinds of home background, whereas *Carrascolendas* serves the particular needs of a minority group, and gives the Mexican-American child a show in which his own ethnic group is represented.

Dual audio television
Other recent American experiments and innovations involving television are less similar to *Sesame Street*. The idea behind 'Dual Audio' television, developed by Terry Borton (8), is to provide a second auditory channel which can increase children's learning from regular commercial programmes. Borton argues that although the average child spends a great deal of time watching television he learns very little from the medium, despite the fact that it exposes the child to an enormous amount of potentially useful information. He thinks that this is partly because much of the information is not in a form in which the young child can adequately

137

perceive and understand it. The language, especially, is often beyond the child's level of comprehension. In addition, television fails to provide the young viewer with opportunities to discover how he can make use of the information he does receive, or with feedback enabling him to check on the adequacy of his understanding. Borton considers that there is a need to provide closer connections between the child's own understanding and the information content that is transmitted on television. The shows that children watch do contain a wide variety of concepts that could be useful to them, and many kinds of knowledge which might be valuable. The problem is to help children benefit from the medium, and learn more than they currently do from the information given on television.

Borton's solution is to provide a secondary auditory channel, serving a number of functions, all of them designed to give the child a better understanding of the non-educational programmes he regularly watches. The second auditory channel reaches the child either via a radio receiver already in the room or via a simple, cheaply-made transistor radio that is equipped with an ear-insert and pre-set on the wavelengths selected for the additional auditory channel. The second channel serves as an addition to the standard one, and not as a substitute for it. The announcer on the second channel makes his comments when there are pauses in the dialogue, and is careful not to interrupt when the television characters are talking.

A variety of useful messages can be transmitted to the children on the second channel. One use is to define or explain words occurring in the original programme. For instance, in Borton's description of an experiment with dual audio based upon *The Dick Van Dyke Show*, the characters talk about writing a 'monologue'. On the second channel the narrator provides a simple definition of this word, just after the first time it is used. When the word is used again in the show the definition is provided once more. On the third occasion the narrator simply repeats the word 'Monologue', to draw the children's attention to it. Essentially the same procedure is followed for other words which the children are not expected to know.

In one episode of an adventure series for which a second auditory channel has been provided, the hero is sent to investigate mysterious activities under the sea. At one point the announcer on the dual channel defines the word 'investigate', telling the children that to investigate means to find out everything you can about something, like solving a mystery. A few minutes later, as the hero begins to discover clues, the

138

dual channel announcer repeats and expands the original definition of 'investigate', noting that the hero must have found a clue in his investigation. Later on, the dual audio narrator finds other ways of making use of the word. For instance, as the hero notices an underwater building the narrator says 'What! A building underwater! Now there's something to find out about, something to investigate.' When some underwater police appear, he suggests that they too must be investigating the mystery. Later still, as the hero resumes his search, and uses a searchlight, the narrator draws attention to it, and asks his listeners whether they have ever used a torch to investigate something.

The repeated definitions and explanations of important words on the extra channel are aimed primarily at promoting vocabulary acquisition in children. Vocabulary is considered to be a crucial component of a child's understanding, and is basic to a variety of learned abilities. For this reason vocabulary development has received considerable emphasis in most dual audio broadcasts designed to accompany everyday television programmes. However, there are a variety of alternative ways in which imaginative use of a second channel might aid the young child. For example, in *The Dick Van Dyke Show* episode mentioned above, one of the characters tells a lie. At this point the dual audio announcer asks the viewers to listen to the character's tone of voice and decide whether or not they believe him. During an argument in the show, the children are asked to take sides. Later, after an ingenious problem-solving procedure has been used in the programme, the narrator draws attention to it, and helps the child audience think about possible applications of it in their own lives.

A dual auditory channel can also be used to take advantage of the opportunities that non-educational television shows make available for helping children who are learning to read. The announcer on the dual channel can help child viewers by reading titles, actors' names and the various signs that appear on the screen in the course of most programmes. On some instances he might just start a phrase, or supply a vowel sound, or the initial consonant of a word.

Sometimes, the second auditory channel may carry explanations of events which the child lacks sufficient knowledge and background information to understand. For example, in one sequence *Batman* is trapped in an ascending balloon which holds a bomb set to explode at 20,000 feet. To escape from his predicament, Batman whistles, whereupon a friendly bird comes along and pecks a hole in the fabric of the balloon. It then begins to descend, removing our hero from danger. This sequence will be largely unintelligible to the child viewer unless he understands why the

139

balloon is descending, and why the bird is significant. The dual audio announcer can aid children who are watching the programme by explaining all this. At the same time he can take the opportunity to define some key words and phrases used in the programme, such as altimeter and bird whistle.

A further role for an additional auditory channel is to induce the young viewer to participate more actively as he watches television. One approach is to get the child to anticipate parts of a programme he is watching, by asking him what he thinks is going to happen next. Another possibility is to ask the viewer whether if he was placed in a similar situation he would have acted differently to the character on the screen. Or the child might be required to imitate one of the characters. Procedures of this kind could make a valuable contribution towards making the experience of watching television less passive, encouraging viewers to participate by thinking, talking and interacting not only with the announcer on the second channel but also with others who are watching television at the same time. In short, imaginative use of a second channel might bring about a substantially altered relationship between the viewer and the environment that television provides.

Unfortunately, there are some practical obstacles to the implementation of dual audio television. For instance, it is not easy to ensure perfect synchronization between the two channels. Apart from this, it is difficult to design second channel contents which do aid learning but which do not result in the child being bombarded with more auditory information than he can process. Furthermore, there are technical problems involved in developing cheap ways of ensuring that a child can easily hear both channels at the same time. On the whole, providing ear-inserts appears to be the most effective way of achieving this. Although dual audio television has the great economic advantage, compared with other innovations, of not having to provide any programmes as such, the production and technical problems associated with producing the second channel are not inconsiderable.

A great deal depends upon the careful designing of material for the second auditory channel, and upon the style and personality of the narrator or announcer. The technical quality of the extra channel must be clear and well synchronized, and the content needs to be lively and interesting; otherwise children just will not bother to turn it on. The developers of dual audio television have been careful to avoid a 'teacher's voice' that might bore or alienate the children, and they have taken pains to find an announcer who conveys warmth, humour, and the sense of a real

140

personality, and who speaks in a language pattern and intonation familiar to and easily understood by the audience for whom the materials are primarily intended, mainly black working-class inner-city children. The intention is to produce the effect of a 'bright and humorous older friend who is watching TV with (the viewer) and helping him'. (9)

The effectiveness of dual audio television has been measured in some small-scale investigations, but the innovation has not yet been subjected to a well-designed large-scale evaluation study such as that developed for *Sesame Street.* Some of the available findings suggest that dual audio can produce at least some of the benefits claimed for it. First, there is little doubt that viewers receiving dual audio are often more active while watching television than viewers who only hear the regular channel. In watching an experiment in which six short television sequences were shown to children those who received an added audio channel made about four times as many comments and gestures than viewers without dual audio and were judged to be responding more enthusiastically and getting more enjoyment out of what they saw. It was also found that children who heard only the original channel made twice as many errors than those who received a dual audio transmission, on tests of vocabulary and knowledge about the programmes. In short, there is little doubt that children can learn more when a second channel is available. The originators of dual audio television have also observed significant positive correlations between amount of dual-audio listening, measured in days, and oral test scores for the vocabulary taught on the second channel. Children aged between seven and eleven who watched *Gilligan's Island* accompanied by a dual audio commentary for ten days were able to define about twice as many of the words explained on the second auditory channel as those who had not listened to dual audio. (9)

Dual-audio television is an interesting new procedure that deserves further investigation. There are a number of ways in which it might be developed. For example it could be extensively utilized in foreign language instruction, for adults as well as children. Another possibility is to provide a substitute channel as a replacement for the original channel rather than as an addition to it. Such a procedure would avoid the danger of having too much auditory information, and sound tracks could be specially produced for particular groups of viewers. Additional or replacement auditory channels could be produced at the same time as the primary channel, using the same production facilities. If this were done, a number of the technical problems would be reduced or eliminated. Such a development would require the cooperation of the

141

television industry, and this might be easier to arrange in Britain than in the United States.

Yet another recent American experiment involving the use of television to teach young children goes by the name of *Pop-Up*. (10) A *Pop-Up* is a short, one-minute film shown on television, replacing one minute of normal transmissions. *Pop-Ups* are made to help children who are learning to read. Their aim is not to make every child an accomplished reader, but simply to give assistance in some basic principles. The fact that *Pop-Ups* are viewed in the safe environment of the home may make them especially valuable for children who are not successful at school. Since they are short the child is not required to sit through a lengthy programme in order to learn, and there is therefore no need to compete with entertainment shows for engaging and maintaining the viewer's prolonged attention. The short, snappy format of television commercials is adapted to the presentation of a number of simple reading principles. The viewer does not have to understand everything on the first occasion he watches a particular *Pop-Up*, because he will eventually see each *Pop-Up* several times or more, just as commercials are seen repeatedly.

It is open to question whether or not materials in the *Pop-Up* kind of format will contribute substantially to children's learning, and firm evidence concerning their effectiveness is not yet available. It seems quite likely that this commercial-like format can make a contribution to teaching some intellectual skills. *Pop-Ups* may well have a useful function, albeit a limited one.

Schools television in BRitain

As I mentioned earlier, British television regularly broadcasts a large number of educational programmes for children. High standards of production are the rule, but information about the effectiveness of the programmes at enabling children to learn is unfortunately sparse. The present state of affairs in British educational television contrasts with that in North America, in that while most of the bolder American experiments involving the use of television have taken place outside the school system, British companies have worked in reasonably close cooperation with the schools, and most educational programmes for children are transmitted during term in school hours.

Schools television programmes are produced by both the BBC and the companies belonging to the Independent Broadcasting Authority. The BBC can draw upon a fifty-year tradition of schools broadcasting by radio. (11) In addition to its production staff the BBC employs around twenty educational officers whose duties include visiting schools to

142

discuss how teachers are making use of the television materials that are provided, and assessing the needs that might be met by programmes to be developed in the future. The field officers provide one useful source of feedback to the BBC concerning the effectiveness of its programmes. On the whole this feedback is more informal and impressionistic than the findings emerging from the quantitative evaluation studies that have been undertaken in the United States. Each approach has distinct advantages and concurrent limitations, and in Britain both are necessary if optimum use is to be made of the medium for educational purposes.

BBC schools television makes use of a good deal of information about teachers' views. In addition to those teachers who communicate directly to the Schools Broadcasting Council and those who are consulted by the educational officers, a large number are asked to answer detailed questionnaires. Their responses are passed on to the producers, most of whom have had teaching experience.

Schools television was initially regarded as a medium for providing enrichment and supplementary educational experiences rather than direct instruction or 'teaching' as such, and to some extent this emphasis has remained. Schools programmes are seen as resources available to the teacher, which are culturally enriching rather than didactive, 'almost educative rather than educational'. (12) But pressing educational needs have led to the provision of some programmes that do offer direct instruction, for instance in the field of mathematics. Mathematics is not a subject well-suited to communication by radio, and at the commencement of schools television in 1957 it received very little attention. Yet it became apparent that there was a serious shortage of mathematics teachers in Britain, especially at the sixth-form level. It was suggested that schools broadcasts in mathematics should be introduced, not just to supplement teaching in schools, but also, in view of the lack of sufficient numbers of teachers, to teach the subject. This was done and has proved reasonably successful, helping large numbers of students to cover the orthodox 'A' Level syllabus.

On the whole, the BBC would rather produce mathematics materials that are less closely tied to the requirements of a particular examination syllabus. The preference is for materials which take full advantage of the audio-visual nature of the television medium. Animated materials and films can be shown, as can large-scale experiments and mechanical and biological models. Television is highly suitable for communicating 'new' topics and those that are visually stimulating.

In the case of modern approaches to mathematics, and other subjects as well, the intention is to aid the teachers who wish to increase their knowledge, as well as the pupils. Television is an ideal medium for disseminating new ideas among teachers, and if this can be done on a regular daily basis, without requiring attendance at special course, so much the better. Teachers are also helped by the provision of 'Teachers' notes', which give advice on ways of ensuring that children benefit as much as possible from educational programmes.

At present the BBC broadcasts around forty schools television programmes per week throughout the twenty-eight weeks of the school broadcasting year. The average length of a programme is twenty minutes. Roughly half of these are aimed at children under eleven years of age. The range of subjects includes English, geography, history, mathematics, modern languages and science, and there are also materials on environmental studies, general humanities, careers and general studies, as well as programmes specially designed for the needs of less able children.

The BBC is aware that providing special programmes for the needs of subnormal or exceptional children is not always desirable. (The favourite television programme of deaf children is *Top of the Pops*!) One programme designed for the deaf, *Vision One,* became much more successful when it developed into a fast-moving visual entertainment for all child viewers. In 1974 to meet the needs of children living in Britain whose ability to use the English language is deficient the BBC introduced *You and Me,* designed for four-and five-year-olds. Older children who are not greatly interested in the relatively academic matters emphasized at school are offered *Scene,* which attempts to help bridge the gap between school and life, to give youngsters a better understanding of their own environment and equip them with knowledge that may help them deal with everyday problems.

The total number of television programmes for schools produced by the independent television companies is just slightly over forty, roughly equivalent to the number provided by the BBC. (13) There is a fair amount of informal cooperation between the individuals responsible for BBC and ITV schools television, and overlapping in programme aims and contents is generally avoided. Schools broadcasting by the independent television companies started in 1957, at the time that BBC Schools Broadcasting Services began using television. Like the BBC, the independent companies employ education officers who visit schools and keep in touch with teachers and local education authorities, in order to check reactions to programmes and discover what new services are required.

The production staff for each programme include individuals with academic, artistic and technical capabilities. For example, the team

144

responsible for a science series, *The World Around Us,* designed for younger children, consisted of the producer, a television director responsible for day-to-day progress, his secretary and assistant, a science teacher who was employed as an education officer, a stage manager and the presenter of the programme. The presenter wrote the script in collaboration with a subject-matter expert serving as a specialist adviser.

Like the BBC, the independent companies produce programmes covering a variety of topics. For example, *You and the World* caters for less academic school leavers. It helps them to look objectively at the differences between school and the world of work, and at the choices they are likely to make. *Believe it or not* and *Have a Heart* provide religious education, a subject which receives less attention in BBC schools television. *Experiment* caters for advanced science students, as *The World About Us* does for younger pupils. *Facts for Life* and *Living and Growing* provide sex and health education, and *Starting Out* explores the world of feeling and the needs of older children growing into adults. Modern languages programmes include *Le Nouvel Arrivé* and *En Français.* Environmental studies are covered by *Images, Let's Look at Ulster, Look Around, Let's Go Out* and *It's Life With David Bellamy.* There are a number of programmes about aspects of history, including *Flashback, The Captured Years, Song and Story, How We Used to Live,* and *History Around Us. Writer's Workshop* and *Over to You* aim to encourage literary and artistic activities in children. A number of series are specifically designed for younger viewers, up to around nine years of age. Two of these, *Figure it Out* and *More Mathman,* provide elementary mathematics. One, *Good Health,* covers health education. Other programmes for younger school viewers include *History Around You, Finding Out, Picture Box, Stop, Look, Listen* and *My World,* which shows the work of essential members of the community, and introduces unfamiliar experiences.

Both the BBC and the independent companies are concerned that schools should be able to take maximum advantage of the schools broadcasting facilities that are offered. A large proportion of schools do make some use of broadcasts, a few series being watched by as many as half of the schools containing pupils in the audience for whom the programmes have been devised, but many programmes are not seen by many of the teachers who might be expected to find them valuable. Much of this apparent under-use may be due to the inadequacy of services for providing liaison between the television companies and the schools. The education officers employed by the BBC and those who work for the independent companies help with this, but their numbers are very small indeed in relation to the vast number of schools in the United Kingdom. British schools number over 32,000, so there is something like one education officer for every thousand schools.

An attempt to help compensate for the paucity of liaison facilities is provided by a short report written by C G Hayter on *Using broadcasting in schools* (14), published jointly by the BBC and ITV in 1974. Some imaginative uses of available services on television are described in the published report, which was produced to communicate ideas and information about using television. Mr Hayter talked to a large number of teachers about their use of schools' television, and he surveyed the findings of a number of individual reports written by teachers who had volunteered to undertake projects. It emerges that teachers vary considerably in the manner in which they make use of the facilities available to them. Typically the broadcasts are used imaginatively as educational components that are closely tied in with other school activities and instruction.

In a number of schools the television project coincided with the introduction of a video-tape recorder. This is a tool that can extend the convenience and utility of schools television services. Teachers are freed from transmission timetables, and once a programme has been recorded, it can be used whenever it is required. Furthermore, parts or all of a programme can be repeated over a short period of time, as and when occasion demands.

Both teachers and children gain much more from televised materials when they are used as part of a carefully planned curriculum than when they serve as an 'extra'. Closer integration of broadcasts and other materials and activities led to greater participation by students, closer observation and more queries and criticisms. Under these conditions television is used as one source of material to serve educational goals, in the same way as are other educational materials, rather than being a loosely connected addition to school life. Considerable planning in advance is necessary if teachers are to make the most effective use of television programmes. This is not always easy, because of practical problems. For example, the 'Teachers' notes' have not always been available until shortly before transmission of a programme, depriving teachers of the detailed knowledge of programme contents that is necessary for planning.

The report includes a number of case studies, giving fairly detailed accounts of how particular schools have made use of television facilities, and showing how these were integrated with other educational materials and learning activities. For instance, one teacher describes the
146

activities of children aged around fourteen, engaged in a brief study of British social history. A major aim was for the pupils to understand how people lived in the early nineteenth century and to appreciate the impact of the Industrial Revolution and its effects on the lives of wealthy and poor families. Only two television programmes were used, 'The Mill Children' and 'Rich and Poor' both of which came from the television series *British Social History*. In addition a radio episode with accompanying slides was incorporated, 'Drift to the Cities', from a series named *History in Focus*. The class also used local sources of evidence that were available in the predominantly industrial locality, plus archive materials and the contents of a Jackdaw folder on Lord Shaftesbury. The teacher, who had seen the television programmes in advance, talked to the children about them before they were shown, and lengthier discussions took place afterwards. During the discussions the children kept returning to the fact that children working up to seventeen hours per day in the mills were younger than them, and this realization helped them appreciate how much better off they were.

In other teaching projects more extensive use was made of television. For instance, one environmental studies course designed for a group of non-academic boys living in a poor industrialized urban region was based on the philosophy that 'hearing is forgetting, seeing is remembering and doing is understanding'. An aim was to get pupils involved in practical activities and field work. Selected educational television episodes were chosen from a number of educational series, *Science Extra, Biology, Science Session, Scene, British Social History* and *Countdown*. Some of the selected programmes were more effective than others, but most led to lively discussions and encouraged further activities. A number of the pupils consequently became involved in large-scale projects, although they had previously been unwilling to undertake activities of this kind. The availability of video tapes gave much-valued flexibility in deciding when to show particular programmes. For example, it was possible to encourage the children to work on outdoor projects whilst the weather was mild, and present the television programmes during a period of bad weather. Television brought a number of benefits. The use of this medium stimulated the boys' interest and awareness, and their understanding of concepts and principles in the field of ecology became much clearer. Outlooks were broadened as the boys began to appreciate the national validity of local studies, and acquired new skills, such as the ability to construct topological maps. Most importantly, television contributed markedly to enjoyment of the activities, and thus helped to bring about a situation more

147

conducive to learning among these boys, who were anything but enthusiastic about the majority of school activities.

As we have seen, British schools programmes differ from most of the American innovations described earlier in that the former were designed to help the teacher educate children, whereas the latter are intended to provide a kind of substitute. For this reason evaluation studies such as those designed for the American programmes would be to some extent out of place with the British materials, most of which are not designed to provide a complete instructional 'package' on their own. Nevertheless there remains a need for quantitative and systematic knowledge about the influence of British schools' television programmes upon the children who watch them, in addition to information which comes from the teachers. Well-designed investigations could yield knowledge about the effects of the programmes for schools that would be highly valuable to teachers, pupils and television producers alike.

REFERENCES

1 Mayer, M: *About television.* New York: Harper and Row, 1972, p 133.

2 Cooney, J G: Sesame Street: the experience of one year. *Television quarterly,* 9, 1970, pp 9–13.

3 Lesser, G S: Learning, teaching and television production for children: the experience of Sesame Street. Pp 265–310 in Dreitzel, H P (ed): *Childhood and socialization.* New York: Macmillan, 1973.

4 Ball, S, and Bogatz, G A: *The first year of Sesame Street: an evaluation.* Princeton, New Jersey: Educational Testing Service, 1970.

5 Ball, S, and Bogatz, G A: Summative research of Sesame Street: implications for the study of preschool children. *Minnesota symposia on child psychology,* 6, 1972, pp 3–17.

6 Diaz-Guerrero, R, and Holtzman, W H: Learning by televised 'Plaza Sesamo' in Mexico. *Journal of educational psychology,* 66, 1974, pp 632–643.

7 Williams, F, and Natalico, Diana S: Evaluating Carrascolendas: a television series for Mexican–American children. *Journal of broadcasting,* 16, 1972, pp 299–309.

8 Borton, T: Dual audio television. *Harvard educational review,* 41, 1974, pp 64–78.

9 Borton, T: Dual audio television: the first public broadcast. *Journal of communication,* in press.
148

10 Klein, P: Pop-Up: a solution to America's reading problem. *Television quarterly*, 9, 1970, pp 26–29.

11 Fawdry, K: School television in the BBC. Pp 13–29 in Moir, G (ed): *Teaching and television*. Oxford: Pergamon, 1973.

12 *Children as viewers and listeners*. London: BBC, 1974.

13 Warren, C: Independent school television—the first ten years. Pp 31–42 in Moir, G (ed): *Teaching and television*. Oxford: Pergamon, 1973.

14 Hayter, C G: *Using broadcasts in schools: a study and evaluation*. London: joint BBC/ITV publication, 1974.

Chapter 7

SOME CONCLUDING REMARKS

The evidence surveyed in the preceding chapters shows conclusively
that television does have a powerful influence on the young. It has both
desirable and undesirable effects. The undesirable outcomes that have
been identified include not only some directly harmful effects of watching television, such as increases in aggressive actions, but also some further
influences which are potentially harmful, such as the misleading view of
human societies that prolonged exposure to the medium instills in many
children.

Realization of the fact that television is a powerful influence in children's lives should encourage all of us to think seriously about how it
ought to be used. However, agreeing that there is a need for concern
should not lead solely to a preoccupation with the policing and controlling of television, in order to purge the medium of materials and malprac-
tices that can be harmful. In the past, concern about television has been
too exclusively focused upon its role as a potential teacher of violence
and delinquency. As some of the investigations surveyed in these pages
have revealed, television can also have a number of beneficial influences
upon children. Quite apart from contributing to their education, and
enabling them to acquire intellectual skills such as those basic to literacy
and numeracy, the medium has been found to have the capacity to help
children acquire some of the social skills and habits that underly cooperation and communication between individuals. Television has also helped
children to acquire the habit of giving persistent and careful attention to
tasks, and this facilitates learning in a variety of situations. Legitimate
concern to limit and prevent the broadcasting of harmful material ought
not to blind us to the numerous ways in which the medium can be valuable to society and to the individual. It might be wise to pay at least as
much attention to the tasks of investigating and measuring the positive
outcomes of using television, and developing better ways of using the
medium for social gain, as is given to undertaking research into the
150

effects of television violence and devising campaigns to protest against aspects considered undesirable.

In Britain we have been wary of using television as an instrument of direct instruction to the young, and perhaps rightly so. Granted that it is desirable to exploit to the full the capacities of any medium which can increase the quality of children's thinking and contribute to their social development, we certainly do not want television as a Big Brother. There are obvious reasons for not wanting any mass medium to become an overly powerful and pervasive influence in children's lives. But in those circumstances in which widespread deficiencies in learning exist and in which television has been proved effective for helping children to acquire the habits, skills, or items of knowledge in which they are deficient, it seems desirable to make use of this particular medium.

There is a widespread and reasonable belief that children's education ought to be left to teachers and parents, rather than being provided by a medium which is necessarily impersonal in some respects, and which is unable to provide certain kinds of individual attention and feedback to the learner. However, accepting that the role of television is limited should not lead to our neglecting the enormous contributions of which it is capable. Furthermore, the proven effectiveness of programmes such as *Sesame Street* in teaching young children some of the skills and abilities which have traditionally been regarded as necessitating the presence of a teacher can encourage us to be open-minded and to be wary of accepting too readily the assumption that television is 'unsuitable' for this or that educational function. In connection with *Sesame Street,* I suspect that some of the highly emotional negative responses it has evoked have been due to its success in showing that television could achieve certain goals for which classroom teachers have customarily been regarded as indispensable, thereby touching a few raw nerves. On more than one occasion I have become involved in discussions with individuals who were strongly attacking this particular programme, only to discover later that the person attacking it had not on any occasion actually seen the programme!

So far as potentially harmful televised materials are concerned it is necessary to take appropriate actions, in order to protect the young. Banning certain programmes is one solution, but it is not always the best one, especially since such a procedure may lead to individuals who would not be harmed by those materials being unnecessarily deprived of them. A good crime series that is enjoyed by many adults might be harmful to some children, but to ban it completely would be undesirable except as a last resort. An alternative solution is to restrict some items to the late evenings, when most children are in bed, and this practice is followed by broadcasting companies in Britain. But even this is a blunt instrument for protecting children, since, as we have mentioned earlier, a surprisingly large number of them are allowed to watch television until late in the evening. These children are likely to be the ones who are most strongly influenced by the medium, and thus most at risk to the deleterious impact of the violent and anti-social models it depicts.

There seems little justification for presenting highly violent materials known to be harmful to some children at times when the young form a majority or a substantial minority of the audience. In my opinion the violent American cartoons shown during the afternoons on British television fall into this category, and ought to be banned. Findings from experimental research have shown the claim that violence in cartoon form is necessarily less influential than 'real' violence to be untrue, and quite apart from the actual violence in these cartoons, the examples they provide of how individuals should interact towards each other are totally undesirable. It is easy for an adult to appreciate that cartoons are not to be taken seriously; young children unfortunately lack the body of knowledge and reasoning skills required for making some of the necessary fine distinctions between reality and the world of cartoons.

The suggestion that particular materials ought not to be permitted on television quite rightly evokes concern about issues of censorship. However, a distinction needs to be made between banning something because it is known to be harmful and banning that involves the suppression of the individual's freedom to express his views. It is doubtful whether forbidding expression of physical violence on television could in many instances be regarded as a hindrance to free expression. There do exist some examples of productions that combine undeniable artistic merit with violent acts that may be harmful. Stanley Kubrick's film 'Clockwork Orange' is a rare instance that comes to mind, and in such a case censorship decisions have to involve the delicate balancing of opposing moral arguments. But instances like this are few, and most of the violent materials currently shown on television are of little artistic value.

There is a need for weapons to protect the young and vulnerable that are more delicate than those of banning programmes or restricting transmission times. A better alternative, insofar as it is possible, is to do more to help children become aware of the nature of the medium, and in particular of the ways in which it can distort important aspects of life, and to equip them to take a more critical and active approach to television. Children and adults need to be 'media conscious' and alive to the

152

manipulative potential of the mass media in general, and especially that of television, as it is the medium that engaged by far the largest proportion of most people's time and attention.

There are a number of ways to help children become more conscious of the possible effects of the medium upon them. One is to involve children in the process of producing television shows, and this has been done in a number of projects undertaken in Britain and in North America. Children have been able to participate in a number of British school- and community-based workshops, and to varying extents in BBC and Independent Television productions. A recent example is the BBC Saturday morning programme *Why Don't You Just Switch Off Your Television And Go And Do Something Less Boring Instead.* In this programme children act as the presenters and they show films and other items they have made. In the United States a well-organised group of adolescents known as The Electric Kids are responsible for the production of a range of televised materials which are seen by large child audiences. In a typical studio production the entire crew is under twenty years of age. They cope with tasks that range from reporting to building studios, writing and camera work. A wide range of programmes is produced, including comedies, talk shows, items covering local events, interviews of celebrities and people of interest. They all make programmes on current problems such as pollution and drug-abuse. The youngsters who participate, contributing on average about eight hours per week, come from a mixture of social and ethnic backgrounds and have a variety of interests and aspirations.

Projects that enable children to learn about television through using the medium themselves can undoubtedly be valuable for the young people concerned, but they tend to be very expensive and thus only available to small numbers. What is really required is to give all child viewers a better awareness of the nature of television. The broadcasting companies themselves are in a good position to help children become more aware of television's influence in their lives, and able to watch actively and critically as they enjoy the medium. There will always be a need for television programmes aimed at making the audience more knowledgeable about the relationship between themselves and the medium, and helping them to become more sensitive to the manner in which it is used and more aware of its incluence upon them. Programmes such as *The Messengers*, which presents extracts from films and television programmes, attempting to show how the visual language of the media can be used to slant or distort the content, and *Viewpoint,* which helps children become more aware of mass media techniques, are helping to meet this need.

Thirty years ago, television was essentially a toy. The vague and often heavily ghosted blue images which flickered on nine-inch screens were an exciting novelty, but television was not the necessary part of many people's daily lives it has subsequently become. Television is now no longer a toy. I have tried to show that it is a force which we have to consider very seriously indeed.

INDEX

155